Another How-To Book

How to Connect With Your Family

MARION HOWARD

Bloomington, IN  Milton Keynes, UK

authorHOUSE™

AuthorHouse™ AuthorHouse™ UK Ltd.
1663 Liberty Drive, Suite 200 500 Avebury Boulevard
Bloomington, IN 47403 Central Milton Keynes, MK9 2BE
www.authorhouse.com www.authorhouse.co.uk
Phone: 1-800-839-8640 Phone: 08001974150

First published by AuthorHouse 4/25/2006

ISBN: 1-4208-7804-2 (sc)

Library of Congress Control Number: 2005908162

Printed in the United States of America
Bloomington, Indiana

This book is printed on acid-free paper.

This book is dedicated to my children ~ Bruce, Judy, Paul,

David, my grandchildren Seth and Josh, and all children with

a curiosity for learning and who like to experiment. It is also

dedicated not only to my family, but also families everywhere

who wish to take an active role in their children's life.

It is my hope that this book will help people to see how important our children are, and how simple it can be to work with them in a creative way that will be positive and fun at the same time. I have used the twelve months of the year as chapter subjects, and have recipes and family activities for each month. Each section will be prefaced with an idea on how to get to know your family in a positive way, and how to have family connections that will be beneficial in life to all members of any family who are willing to take the time to share with each other. Sharing ideas, talents, philosophies, life experiences, and much more is so important in today's society. What better way to get to know each other and to create something that all can enjoy than working together in the kitchen?

This book will combine cooking with lots of ideas on how to work as a family, and a reminder of how important family values are at all times. By working together in the kitchen family members can learn about each other through CONVERSATION while having fun. Sounds like a very simple and easy task, but how many parents, grandparents, or whatever your role is in a child's life actually take the time and energy to see to it that at an early age our children become familiar with the kitchen and what is in it? Why do we have a kitchen, and what part does it have at the core of all families?

The recipes found in the book have been gathered from friends, family, newspaper food sections, clippings from magazines, and from what I call regional cookbooks. These are cookbooks that are published by various community groups as a fund raising project. Whenever you have an opportunity to purchase a cookbook that has recipes from various people who belong to a service organization, it is well worth looking at and possibly purchasing the book. The recipes are usually great and you will be helping some group to fund their favorite projects to help others.

Connecting with your family in a non-threatening way and having fun at the same time can be a challenge. A challenge that can be met in a very subtle and familiar place found in every home. The place: THE KITCHEN. Yes, the kitchen can be one of the best areas in your home to learn together and have a wonderful time and experience as a family.

This book has been a long time coming, and I would like to thank my family and friends for encouraging me along the way. A special thanks to my son for that extra push to make me see it through. I would also like to thank him for helping me put it together in a format that made it possible for me to send it to a publisher.

A special thanks to my husband, Jim, for illustrating the book for me. Without his help and support this would not have happened.

Author ~ Marion Howard

TABLE OF CONTENTS

1 ~ January ~ Salads

"Each one of us obtains in his schooling something which
not he, but the community has paid for. We must return it to
the community in full, in the shape of good citizenship."

~ Theodore Roosevelt

JANUARY ~ SALADS

Salads are refreshing, and can be used for lunches, desserts, and sometimes the main course for a meal.

January always brings the concept of evaluating the years that have gone by in our lives, and the tradition of making New Year's resolutions. New Year's resolutions are something most of us think about and then we either make the resolutions or we don't. Many who do have forgotten them by the end of February, or we wonder why we made them in the first place.

The next time January rolls around, consider a resolution that will last for the entire year on a regular basis. Most of us live in an area that is in need of people who are concerned about their community and want to make it a better place for all to live. Next time January comes, consider volunteering in an area that is of interest to you. It doesn't matter if as a student we need extra help in a certain area at school, or we need extra support when a family problem comes along, or that extra hug when we feel down for one reason or another. It is always great to know that we can find someone who cares enough to help us with whatever situation arises in our lives.

Volunteering is a wonderful way to get to know each other and to help your community grow. No matter what your interest is there is someplace for you to volunteer and make a difference in your life and the lives of those you touch. Do you like animals, reading, park areas around you, politics, or just helping others? If you answered yes to any of these suggestions there is a place in the world of volunteering for you.

Another New Year's resolution to consider is working in the kitchen with your children. What better place to get to know your children than in the kitchen where you work together and then you can share your accomplishments with others. Volunteering is a great family activity and if you did spend time in the kitchen with your children you could then share with others what you have made. Visiting people who live alone, the elderly, a thank you for a next door neighbor, a new neighbor, or anyone who might like some company for a few minutes are great ways to share your time and talents.

I hope that every New Year is a great one for you and your families, and that in the future you consider making resolutions that involve the entire family.

GRAPEFRUIT - COTTAGE CHEESE

1 (3 ounce) package lime jello
juice plus ice water for the jello

½ cup cottage cheese
1 can grapefruit sections (drained)

Mix the jello according to the directions using the grapefruit juice in place of cold water. If there is not 1 cup of juice add cold water to equal 1 cup. Put an ice cube in the juice to make sure it is really cold, this will make the jello set faster. Be sure to remove the ice cube if it does not melt when you put it into the jello.

When the jello is almost set, fold in the cottage cheese and grapefruit sections. Then place in a mold or square pan and refrigerate until set.

BEAN SALAD AND DRESSING

⅓ cup oil
1 tablespoon sage

¼ cup red wine vinegar
1 clove garlic finely chopped

Mix the above ingredients and refrigerate several hours before using.

1 can wax beans
1 can kidney beans
⅓ cup chopped onions

1 can string beans
1 can garbanzo beans

Mix the above ingredients, and mix with dressing. Chill several hours or overnight before serving.

GREEN SALAD

Green salads can be a mixture of various lettuces, and any raw vegetable that you might want to add. Carrots, tomatoes, cabbage, peppers; just use your imagination. Following are some dressings that you can use with any green salad. Vegetables should be shredded or cut into bite size pieces.

DRESSINGS:

ITALIAN CHEESE DRESSING

¼ teaspoon celery salt
1 can tomato soup
¼ cup vinegar
¼ cup parmesan cheese
1 teaspoon oregano leaves

¼ cup bleu cheese
½ cup salad or olive oil
1 teaspoon basil leaves
1 clove garlic cut in half

In a covered jar combine ingredients then chill. Shake well before using. Serve with tossed green salad.

ZESTY FRENCH DRESSING

1 can tomato soup
¼ cup vinegar
1 tablespoon finely chopped onion
½ teaspoon salt

½ cup salad or olive oil
2 tablespoons sugar
2 teaspoons dry mustard
¼ teaspoon pepper

In a covered jar combine ingredients, then chill. Shake well before using. Serve with green salad.

BLEU CHEESE DRESSING

1 cup IMO
1 clove garlic, pressed
½ teaspoon salt

1 cup mayonnaise
1 tablespoon lime juice
¼ cup bleu cheese

Mix all ingredients except cheese and stir until smooth. Crumble bleu cheese and stir into mixture. Refrigerate.

GREEN GODDESS DRESSING

1 cup IMO
1 avocado
3 tablespoons chopped parsley
1 clove garlic minced
½ teaspoon salt
⅛ teaspoon pepper

½ cup mayonnaise
3 teaspoons tarragon vinegar
2 teaspoon anchovy paste
1 teaspoon Worcestershire sauce
½ teaspoon dry mustard

Combine all ingredients in blender; blend until smooth. Chill at least 2 hours.

MARINATED CARROTS

2 pounds carrots, sliced thin
1 teaspoon salt
garlic powder
1 (10¾ ounce) can tomato soup
¾ cup white wine vinegar

¾ cup sugar
½ cup oil
1 can sliced water chestnuts
1 bell pepper, seeded and chopped fine
3 green onions or 1 leek chopped fine

Cook carrots in salt water. Do not overcook; you want them to be al-dente. Drain and cool. Add salt, pepper, and a little garlic powder to carrots. Put soup, vinegar, sugar and oil in blender 3 or 4 minutes. Pour over carrots and add remaining vegetables. Mix lightly. Best if made a day before. Keep in refrigerator. Serves 10 to 15 people.

COLE SLAW ~ CRUNCHY

1 head cabbage shredded (can mix
  red and green cabbage, if desired)
4 green onions, chopped
4 teaspoons sesame seeds (optional)

1 can water chestnuts, chopped
  or ½ cup toasted almonds, chopped
1 package dry chicken flavor
Top Ramen noodles broken into small pieces;
  save seasoning for dressing

Combine in large bowl shredded cabbage, green onions, sesame seeds, water chestnuts, toasted almonds and noodles. Toss with dressing before serving.

DRESSING:

4 tablespoons sugar
4 tablespoons vinegar
1 package seasoning from noodles

1 cup vegetable oil
salt to taste
Pepper to taste

Combine all ingredients. Mix well. (If you wish to make salad ahead of time, wait until serving time to add noodles and nuts or they will be too moist.)

SPINACH SALAD

1½ pounds fresh spinach
1 (5 ounce) can water chestnuts drained and sliced
2 hard cooked eggs sliced
½ pound bean sprouts

⅓ cup onions finely chopped
Pinch of salt and pepper
5 slices bacon, cooked
  and crumbled

Mix the above ingredients and toss together.

DRESSING

⅔ cup oil
⅓ cup catsup

2 teaspoons Worcestershire sauce
⅓ cup red wine vinegar

Mix the above ingredients thoroughly and pour over salad.

PICNIC POTATO SALAD

6 medium potatoes boiled in skins
½ cup chopped green onions
2 cups grated cheddar cheese

2 cups sour cream or substitute
1 cube melted butter
Salt and pepper to taste

Preheat over to 350°. Pare and chop the potatoes; add the other ingredients and mix well. Put in casserole and dot top with more butter. Bake for 45 minutes. May serve hot or cold once baked.

SEA FOOD SALAD

1 envelope plain gelatin
¼ cup water
¼ cup boiling water
1 cup celery
3 hard cooked eggs
3 to 4 sweet pickles, chopped
    (May use pickle relish)

1 small bottle pimiento
2 small green onions, chopped
1 cup pastry cream, whipped
1 cup mayonnaise
¼ teaspoon white pepper
 juice of 1 lemon
1 pound small shrimp

Mix gelatin in cold water. Add boiling water. Stir until smooth. Set aside. Combine and mix together celery, eggs, pickles, pimiento, green onions, pastry cream, mayonnaise, white pepper, lemon juice, and shrimp. Add gelatin. Put in 9x13 inch glass baking dish. Refrigerate.

Topping:

1 package raspberry gelatin
1 cup hot tomato juice

1 cup cold tomato juice

Dissolve raspberry gelatin in hot tomato juice. Add cold tomato juice. When cool, spoon carefully over firm salad. Yields 12-16 servings.

MOLDED CUCUMBER SALAD

1 (3 ounce) package lemon jello
1 cup cottage cheese
¾ cup grated cucumber
⅓ cup toasted slivered almonds

¾ cup boiling water
2 tablespoons grated onion
dash of salt
1 cup mayonnaise or salad dressing

Dissolve jello in boiling water. Stir in remaining ingredients and blend well. Pour into 3 to 4 cup mold. Refrigerate until firm then remove from mold.

YANKEE DOODLE SALAD

4 ounces elbow macaroni
1 cup sour cream
¼ cup sweet pickle relish, drained
¼ cup green pepper, chopped
1 green onion, chopped

3 tablespoons vinegar
2 teaspoons prepared mustard
2 cups cheddar cheese, cubed
1 pound hot dogs cut into ½ inch pieces

Cook macaroni according to package directions, then drain. In a large bowl, toss macaroni with sour cream, pickle relish, green pepper, onion, vinegar and mustard. Fold in cheese and hot dog pieces. Chill 3-4 hours to blend flavors.

OVERNIGHT LETTUCE SALAD

1 head lettuce, torn into bite size pieces,
   drained and sliced
½ cup chopped celery
½ cup chopped green pepper
1 small red onion, chopped
1 (10 ounce) package frozen peas, thawed

1 (8½ ounce) can water chestnuts,
1 cup thinly sliced radish
1 cup mayonnaise or salad dressing
1 cup grated parmesan cheese
6 slices crisp bacon, crumbled

Layer lettuce, celery, green pepper, onion, peas, water chestnuts and radishes in a large salad bowl. Spread mayonnaise over the top, sealing layer completely. Cover with plastic wrap and refrigerate. Sprinkle with cheese and bacon, garnish with radish slices if desire. Toss before serving.

11 ~ FEBRUARY ~ DESSERTS

"Do all the good you can. By all the means you can. In all the ways you can. In all the places you can. At all the times you can. To all the people you can. As long as ever you can."

~ John Wesley

FEBRUARY ~ DESSERTS

*Desserts are fun to make and can be a delightful end to any meal.
Depending on what has been served for lunch or dinner will have an
influence on what type of dessert is served. Desserts can vary from a dish
of ice cream or sherbet to a mouth-watering cake, pie, pudding, etc.*

The middle of February is a time we set aside to honor the Presidents of the United States, February 12, 1809, was Abraham Lincoln's birthday, and February 22, 1732, was George Washington's birthday, our sixteenth and first President. Both of these men were an important influence in the history of our country. It is important to reflect on these men as well as the other Presidents who have served our country. In February we have a day to honor all men who have served as Presidents. Have a family project and pick out a President you would like to know more about, then go to the library or internet and do some research and learn more about this great country and the men who were our leaders.

Another day we celebrate this month on February 14th is Valentine's Day. This is a day to show our love and appreciation for those we know and care about. In the community where I live during the week of Valentine's Day we have a week dedicated to RAK, "Random Acts of Kindness." This has become a very important week in our community, and is a time we show others through kindness how important they are to us. It can be very rewarding to do something for someone on a random basis and not let them know who did it. Or it can be an act of kindness that the other person knows about by showing them that you care about them and want to see them smile and be happy. Whatever you do during RAK week let someone know you care about them, everybody likes to feel special.

In February make cards and special treats throughout the month to give at random. Make your own card out of construction paper decorated with ribbons, lace, stickers, or whatever you can find around the house that you think might look great on a card. It is a fun activity and you can send it to that special somebody. If you are ambitious you can use one of the following recipes to send along with the card. If you try one of these recipes be sure that there is an adult around to help you with your kitchen creation.

PINEAPPLE UPSIDE DOWN CAKE

3 eggs, separated
5 tablespoons juice from pineapple
1 cup sugar
1 cup flour

1 teaspoon baking powder
¾ cup margarine or butter
¼ cup brown sugar
1 can sliced pineapple

Beat the egg whites until stiff, set aside. Then beat egg yolks, juice, sugar, flour, and baking powder together. Fold in the egg whites. Melt the margarine, or butter, and brown sugar in a cast iron fry pan or a round cake pan. Place the pineapple slices over the melted margarine and sugar and then gently pour the batter into the pan.

Bake 325° for 40 to 50 minutes. Test with cake tester or toothpick. Turn the cake onto a serving plate and let it cool. Serve with whipped cream or a scoop of ice cream, or plain. Apricots or peaches may also be used. Use canned fruit.

FOUR LAYER DESSERT

1½ sticks margarine
1¼ cup flour
1 cup nuts chopped (optional)
1 (8 ounce) package cream cheese
1 cup powdered sugar

8 ounces non-dairy whip
1 small package instant vanilla pudding
1 small package instant chocolate pudding
3 cups milk

Preheat oven to 350°. Melt margarine; mix with flour and nuts. Press in a 9x13 inch baking dish. Bake for 25 minutes. Cool.

Layer 2: Blend cream cheese and powdered sugar. Fold in 4 ounces non-dairy whip. Spread over first layer.

Layer 3: Mix both pudding mixes together with milk. Spread on second layer.

Layer 4: Top with 4 ounces non-dairy whip. Spread on third layer. Refrigerate.

CARROT CAKE

3 cups all purpose unbleached flour
3 teaspoons baking soda
2 teaspoons cinnamon
½ teaspoon salt
2 cups carrots, shredded
1½ cups flaked coconut

⅔ cup vegetable oil
1½ cups molasses
1 (8¼ ounce) can crushed pineapple
  (in heavy syrup, do not drain)
¾ cup golden raisins
½ cup pecans, chopped (Any nut will do)

Preheat oven to 350°. Combine all ingredients except raisins and pecans. Blend well. Add raisins and pecans. Pour batter into greased baking pan. Bake for 35 to 45 minutes or until cake is firm to touch. Use a 9 x13 inch pan. Cool completely. Frost.

FROSTING

3 cups powdered sugar (more if needed)
1 (8 ounce) package cream cheese softened

2 teaspoons margarine or butter softened
1 teaspoon vanilla

Combine all ingredients together. Blend until smooth. Frost carrot cake.

GERMAN CHOCOLATE CAKE

1 package German chocolate cake mix
1 can cherry pie filling

1 teaspoon almond flavoring
2 eggs beaten

Preheat oven to 350°. Put all ingredients into a large bowl and mix with a large spoon, fold together until it is well mixed. Pour into a 9x13 inch greased and floured pan. Bake for 50 to 55 minutes. Serve with powdered sugar, butter frosting, or whipped cream.

EASY DUMP CAKE

1 package Yellow cake mix
1 large can crushed pineapple (Do not drain)
1 can cherry pie filling

½ cup chopped nuts
1 cube margarine

Preheat oven to 350°. Butter a 13x9x2 inch baking pan. Spread the dry cake mix evenly over the bottom of the pan. Pour pineapple over evenly. Spoon cherry pie filling over this, and then add nuts. Dot the top with margarine in squares. Do not stir. Bake 1 hour.

PUMPKIN PIE CAKE

4 eggs beaten
1 (29 ounce) can pumpkin
1½ cups sugar
2 teaspoons cinnamon
1 teaspoon ginger

½ teaspoon cloves
1 yellow cake mix
½ pound butter or margarine, melted
1 cup sliced almonds or walnuts
whipped cream or non-dairy whip

Preheat over to 350°. Mix all ingredients thoroughly, except cake mix, melted butter, nuts and topping. Pour into greased 9x12 inch pan. Sprinkle dry cake mix evenly over top of pumpkin mixture. Sprinkle almonds or walnuts over cake mix. Drizzle melted butter over nuts and cake mixture. Bake 50 to 60 minutes. Top with whipped cream or non-dairy whip.

PIE CRUST

4 cups all purpose flour
1¾ cups vegetable shortening
1 tablespoon sugar
1 teaspoon salt

1 tablespoon vinegar
1 egg
½ cup ice water

With fork, mix together first 4 ingredients. In a separate dish, beat remaining ingredients. Combine the two mixtures stirring with fork until moistened. Mix with hands and mold into two balls. Chill for 15 minutes before rolling. Dough can be refrigerated up to 3 days or frozen until ready to use. Yields 2 (9 inch) crusts.
Note: Dough will remain soft in refrigerator and can be taken out and rolled at once.

PUMPKIN PIE FILLING

3 cups pumpkin (canned)
1½ cups sugar
1 teaspoon salt
1 teaspoon ginger
2 teaspoons cinnamon

½ teaspoon nutmeg
½ teaspoon cloves
6 eggs slightly beaten
2½ cups milk
1⅓ cups evaporated milk

(Or use 3 teaspoons pumpkin pie spice and 1 teaspoon cinnamon instead of ginger, cinnamon, nutmeg and cloves.)

Thoroughly combine pumpkin, sugar, salt, and spices. Add eggs, milk and evaporated milk, and mix well. Pour into 9 inch pastry lined pie pan (Have edges crimped high). Bake in oven at 350° for 1 hour or until knife inserted comes out clean. Yields 2 (9 inch) pies.

STRAWBERRY GLAZED PIE

1 cup water	2 tablespoons orange juice
¼ cup strawberry jelly	(9 inch) pie shell baked (or crumb crust)
3 ounce package strawberry jello	1 quart fresh strawberries
2 (3 ounce) packages cream cheese softened	non-dairy whip
1 tablespoon sugar	

Heat water and jelly in small saucepan over high heat until it boils and jelly is melted. Add gelatin then stir until dissolved. Refrigerate or place in ice water until mixture mounds slightly when dropped from a spoon. Beat cream cheese, add sugar and orange juice. Beat until fluffy. Spread in a 9 inch baked pie shell. Arrange fresh strawberries on top. Spoon glaze mixture over the berries. Cover with non-dairy whip.

CRUMB CRUST

1½ cups finely crushed corn flakes	⅓ cup melted butter
½ cup finely chopped nuts	½ teaspoon cinnamon (optional)
⅓ cup sugar	¼ teaspoon nutmeg (optional)

Combine all ingredients and press into pie pan or spring form pan. This is excellent for gelatin and non-dairy whip pies. Save ½ cup of topping for top of pie.

JELLO CAKE

1 package yellow cake mix	¾ cup water
1 package lemon jello	¾ cup salad oil

Mix all the cake ingredients together about 2 minutes. Pour into greased and floured 9 x 13 inch pan. Bake at 350° for 35 minutes. While cake is still hot, poke holes all over with a fork and loosen edges. Pour glaze over hot cake.

Glaze:

1½ cups powdered sugar	juice of 2 lemons

Mix thoroughly and pour over cake.

LEMON STREUSEL CAKE

1 package lemon cake mix with pudding	3 eggs
1 cup plain yogurt	1 cup finely chopped walnuts or almonds
⅓ cup vegetable oil	⅓ cup brown sugar, packed
¼ cup water	1 teaspoon ground cinnamon

Preheat oven to 325°. Grease and flour 9 x 13 inch pan.
Reserve 2 tablespoons of the cake mix (dry). Beat remaining cake mix, the yogurt, oil, water and eggs on low speed for 30 seconds to mix. Beat on medium speed for 2 minutes.

Mix walnuts, brown sugar, cinnamon and reserved cake mix. Pour half of the batter into pan. Sprinkle with half of the walnut mixture. Repeat with remaining batter and walnut mixture. Bake 40 to 45 minutes or until toothpick inserted in center comes out clean. Cool. Serve with ice cream or whipped cream if desired.

BUTTER FROSTING

⅓ cup butter, margarine, or shortening	2 cups sifted confectioners sugar
About ¼ cup milk or cream	1½ teaspoons vanilla

With an electric mixer cream the butter. Add 1 cup sugar and beat until light and fluffy. Add remaining sugar and milk alternately, beating until very smooth and creamy. Add vanilla. Frosts center and sides of a two layer cake.

For a CHOCOLATE BUTTER FROSTING add 3 squares melted unsweetened chocolate to butter.

BAKED APPLES WITH LEMON SAUCE

Apples	Prepared Mincemeat

Select large baking apples. Core the apple ½ of the way through from the stem being careful not to cut through to the bottom, fill centers with prepared mincemeat. Place in baking dish. Add hot water to a depth of about ¼ inch. Cover baking dish. Bake at 350° for 45 to 50 minutes or until tender. Serve warm with lemon sauce.

LEMON SAUCE

2 eggs	⅔ cup sugar
½ cup milk	6 tablespoons melted butter
Grated peel of 1 lemon	2 tablespoons lemon juice

Beat eggs until light, add sugar gradually, beat until fluffy. Stir in remaining ingredients. Cook over hot water stirring constantly until mixture coats spoon. Serve warm.

III ~ MARCH ~ EATING LIGHT

All of us are born for a reason, but all of us don't discover why.
Success in life has nothing to do with what you gain in life
or accomplish for yourself. It's what you do for others.

~ Danny Thomas

MARCH ~ EATING LIGHT

There is a lot of concern lately that the youth of today are overweight. This is a very important issue, which needs to be addressed. One of the main issues is the fact that our children in today's society spend far too much time in front of the TV. They are exposed to not only the program they are watching, but the advertising that is influencing their lives in ways that we don't really think about too much.

The programs being watched deal with a subject matter for 30 to 60 minutes and usually then it is on to some other topic that sometimes carries over to the next episode, and at other times on to an entirely different scenario. Advertising, on the other hand, is repeated time after time in the program being watched, and then again on following programs being repeated over and over. Eventually, those watching will pay attention and either rejects or goes out and buys the product.

What types of foods are being seen on the TV advertising circuit? For the most part the foods are those that have a pleasant appearance and taste, but have little value when it comes to keeping the body healthy. When was the last time you saw an advertisement suggesting that you go to your local grocery store and check out what is in the produce department? Or how about the advertisement of any food that takes a little time to prepare but helps to keep you healthy and fit? Unless you are watching the infomercials which are selling products (not food). TV ads are aimed at the fast food market for those who are in a hurry.

If we are truly going to take an interest in what our children are eating and how what they are eating is affecting them, we must take the time to teach them the importance of good healthy eating! Good and healthy are not words that are particularly popular, but it is important that everyone is made aware of what is happening and how food affects their mental and physical abilities. Let's put on a campaign to educate our children about what they are eating and how to prepare food, and then let them choose which direction they want to take. Will it be fast food from TV advertising, or will it be food that can taste and look absolutely great, and also will help them to be more active both physically and mentally? Food does affect the body and the mind. Cooking at home is important because the ingredients and size of eating portions can be controlled, and the side benefit is that the family can cook together and then enjoy what has been cooked in a relaxed situation.

There are many recipes for light eating, and there will be a few in this chapter. These are suggestions that will get you started, from here just use your imagination and think light when you are preparing a recipe or snack or whatever.

There are several ways you can eat light without using any special recipes. One solution is eating lots of vegetables, broccoli, cauliflower, cabbage, and turnips, to name a few. Vegetables taste quite sweet when they are not cooked at all. Slice raw vegetables and serve them with a dressing. Some suggestions are turnips, jicama, broccoli, cucumber, and the usual standbys like celery, carrots, radishes and mushrooms. Arrange these attractively on a platter and serve with a low-cal dip or your favorite low-cal dressing. (Try making your own dressing to use for this purpose.) This is an excellent way to stave off hunger until dinner, or as the vegetable for a main meal. If cooking vegetables be sure and not overcook them, they taste much better if not overcooked. Steaming vegetables is great because the nutrients aren't lost in boiling water.

Another important thing is not to overeat. When serving your plate keep the portions moderate, and take your time eating. Don't be in a hurry, and relax so you can enjoy the food instead of just eating to be eating. When you take your time eating you will eat less.

CHICKEN CASSEROLE

2¾ cups spiral pasta
½ cup chopped onion
½ cup chopped celery
2 garlic cloves, minced
1 tablespoon olive oil
2 cups cooked chicken breast
1 (10¾ ounce) can
  reduced fat-reduced sodium
  cream of chicken soup, undiluted

1½ cups fat free milk
1 (16 ounce) package Italian blend vegetables
1 cup shredded reduced fat cheddar cheese
2 tablespoons minced fresh parsley
1 teaspoon thyme
¼ teaspoon salt
⅔ cups crushed cornflakes

Cook pasta according to package directions. Meanwhile in a nonstick skillet sauté onion, celery and garlic in oil until tender. Drain pasta then place in a bowl. Add the onion mixture, chicken soup, milk, thawed vegetables, cheese, parsley, thyme, and salt.

Pour into a shallow 3 quart baking dish coated with a nonstick cooking spray. Cover and bake at 350° for 25 minutes. Sprinkle with cornflakes. Bake, uncovered, 7 minutes longer or until heated through.

LENTIL BARLEY STEW

½ cup chopped celery
3 garlic cloves, minced
⅓ cup onion
1 tablespoon butter
3 cups tomato juice
2½ cups seeded and chopped plum tomatoes
1½ cups water

¾ cups dried lentils, rinsed
½ cup pearl barley
½ teaspoon salt
½ teaspoon dried rosemary, crushed
½ teaspoon pepper
½ cup shredded carrot
¾ cup shredded reduced fat
  cheddar cheese

In a large saucepan, sauté celery, garlic and onion in butter until tender. Add the tomato juice, tomatoes, water, lentils, barley and seasonings. Bring to a boil. Reduce heat; cover and simmer for 45 minutes. Add carrots cook 10 minutes longer or until barley and lentils are tender. Sprinkle with cheese.

GARDEN SPAGHETTI

1 tablespoon olive oil	3 cloves garlic
½ pound fresh broccoli, broken into pieces	2 tablespoons all purpose flour
1½ cups sliced zucchini	2 teaspoons chicken bouillon granules
1½ cups sliced mushrooms	1 teaspoon thyme
1 large carrot	2 cups milk
8 ounces uncooked spaghetti	½ cup shredded swiss cheese
2 tablespoons butter or margarine	½ cup shredded mozzarella cheese
¼ cup chopped onion	

In a large skillet, sauté the broccoli, zucchini, mushrooms and carrot in oil until crisp and tender. Remove from the heat and set aside. Cook spaghetti according to package directions. In another saucepan, sauté onion and garlic in butter until tender. Stir in the flour, bouillon and thyme until blended. Gradually add milk. Bring to a boil; cook and stir for 2 minutes or until thickened. Reduce heat to low; stir in cheeses until melted. Add the vegetables then heat through. Drain spaghetti toss with vegetable mixture.

VEGETABLE SOUP

2 leeks (with 1 inch of green left on)	8 ripe plum tomatoes, peeled
4 carrots, diced	or 1 (28 ounce) can plum tomatoes
3 parsnips	6 red potatoes cut into 1 inch pieces
2 tablespoons minced garlic	1 teaspoon dried tarragon
2 tablespoons butter	½ teaspoon ground nutmeg
2 tablespoons olive oil	¼ cup chopped parsley
4 cups vegetable broth	salt and pepper to taste

Clean, trim and finely dice leeks, carrots and parsnips. Combine in a bowl with garlic. Melt the butter with the oil in a large heavy pot over low heat. Add the diced vegetables and cook, stirring occasionally until wilted, about 10 minutes. Add the broth, potatoes, tarragon and nutmeg then cook covered for 15 minutes. Uncover and cook 15 minutes more to enrich the broth. Sprinkle parsley on top before serving.

MEATLESS SIDE DISH

1 clove garlic, minced	1 tablespoon olive oil
2 cups broccoli florets	2 cups cauliflowerets
¼ cup water	¼ teaspoon salt
dash of pepper	

In a large nonstick skillet, sauté garlic in oil for 1 minute. Add the remaining ingredients. Bring to a boil. Reduce heat; cover and simmer for 8 minutes or until tender.

BEEF CASSEROLE

½ pound ground beef
1 medium onion, chopped
1 (28 ounce can) whole peeled tomatoes
  (Drained and chopped)
¾ pound zucchini sliced
parmesan cheese

1 tablespoon olive oil
1 green pepper chopped
1 clove garlic minced
½ teaspoon oregano
2 ounces Linguine or other pasta
  (Cooked al dente)

In pan, sauté ground beef in oil until lightly browned. Drain excess fat. Add onion, green pepper, tomatoes, garlic and oregano cook until thick. Arrange zucchini slices on bottom and sides of shallow 1 quart baking dish; top with cooked pasta. Cover with meat sauce then sprinkle with cheese. Bake in preheated 375° oven for 25 minutes.

SEAFOOD SAUCE

1 cup low calorie mayonnaise
1 tablespoon lemon juice
1 teaspoon horseradish
2 tablespoons plain yogurt

¼ cup tomato sauce
2 tablespoons chopped parsley or chives
1 teaspoon Worcestershire sauce

Combine all ingredients and store sauce in screw top jar in refrigerator. Arrange your choice of seafood on a bed of lettuce and top with sauce. This is good with crabmeat, shrimp, or tuna packed in water for a seafood salad.

STRAWBERRIES WITH RASPBERRY SAUCE

1 quart fresh strawberries
juice of ½ lemon

2 tablespoons honey
10 ounces frozen raspberries

Wash, dry and hull strawberries. Thaw raspberries and combine with the honey and lemon juice and whirl in blender to make a sauce. Serve strawberries, or any combination of favorite berries topped with sauce.

SPAGHETTI SQUASH

1 spaghetti squash, about 3½ pounds
(pierce squash with a fork in several places)
¼ cup olive oil
1 onion, halved lengthwise and slivered
1 red bell pepper and 2 yellow bell peppers
   (cut into ½ inch strips lengthwise)
½ teaspoon salt

¼ teaspoon black pepper
2 ripe tomatoes, peeled, seeded and
   chopped
½ teaspoon sugar
½ cup coarsely torn fresh basil leaves

Preheat oven to 375°. Dry the squash and place in baking pan; bake for 40 minutes. Turn it over and bake 15 to 30 minutes more or until completely tender. Turn off oven and let squash sit while sauce cooks.

Place the olive oil in large, heavy pot over medium-low heat. Add the onion and cook to wilt for 10 minutes, stirring occasionally. Add the peppers then season with salt and pepper. Cover and cook over medium heat, stirring, occasionally, for 20 minutes. Add the tomatoes, sugar and basil; cook uncovered for 10 minutes, stirring. Raise the heat if the tomatoes release too much liquid. Adjust the seasonings and keep warm.

Halve squash lengthwise; discard seeds. Pull apart strands with a fork. Pile into a large shallow bowl and top with the bell pepper sauce.

SWEET AND SOUR ZUCCHINI

2 tablespoons olive oil
2 cloves garlic chopped finely
3 tablespoons raisins
salt and freshly ground pepper to taste

1 large onion chopped
2 pounds zucchini thinly sliced
3 tablespoons wine vinegar
3 tablespoons almonds

In olive oil sauté onion until it's slightly golden. Add garlic and stir. Add zucchini and cook, stirring occasionally, for about 5 minutes. Then add remaining ingredients, except almonds, and cook gently on low for 5 more minutes.

While this is simmering, sauté almonds in olive oil until lightly browned. Add to the zucchini just before serving. Stir well.

PINEAPPLE CHEESE SALAD MOLD

2 cups canned pineapple juice
2 envelopes plain gelatin
1 (8¼ ounce) can crushed pineapple
1 cup small curd cottage cheese

1 cup plain yogurt
3 tablespoons lemon juice
1 teaspoon honey
watercress

Sprinkle gelatin over 1 cup pineapple juice to soften. Stir over low heat until dissolved, reserve ½ cup and set aside. Combine remaining gelatin mixture with remaining 1 cup pineapple juice and undrained crushed pineapple. Chill until it begins to thicken. Turn into 6 cup mold. Chill until softly set. Combine cottage cheese, yogurt, lemon juice and honey. Stir in remaining ½ cup gelatin mixture. If necessary, reheat to liquefy. Spoon over fruit layer in mold. Chill at least 3 hours until firm. Unmold and garnish with watercress.

COTTAGE CHEESE DIP

1 pint cottage cheese
¼ cup finely chopped green pepper
¼ cup finely chopped green chilies
¼ cup finely chopped radishes

1 teaspoon minced onion
¼ teaspoon pepper
¾ teaspoon oregano

For a raw vegetable dip combine cottage cheese, finely chopped green pepper, finely chopped green chilies, finely chopped radishes, minced onion, pepper and oregano. Mix well. Serve with crackers or vegetables.

FRUIT KABOBS WITH PINEAPPLE DIP

Pineapple Dip (below)
30 seedless green grapes
30 pineapple chunks (¼ pineapple), each about ¾ inch wide or
1 can sliced pineapple drained and each slice cut into eight.
30 mandarin orange segments or 1 can mandarin orange segments, drained
15 strawberries cut in half.

Prepare Pineapple Dip. Place any combinations of fruit on plastic or wooden toothpicks. Serve with Pineapple Dip.

PINEAPPLE DIP

1 (8 ounce) package light cream cheese softened
1 cup fat free plain yogurt
2 tablespoons honey
3 teaspoons crushed gingerroot
1 (8½ ounce) can crushed pineapple in juice, drained.

Beat cream cheese, yogurt, honey and gingerroot in medium bowl until creamy. Fold in pineapple. Cover and refrigerate at least 1 hour or until chilled. Cover and refrigerate any remaining dip.

TOMATO PASTA

⅓ cup light olive oil
1 large clove garlic (finely chopped)
A few red pepper flakes
salt and ground pepper to taste

1½ pounds ripe tomatoes (peeled, seeded and chopped)
1 cup fresh basil (coarsely chopped)
1 pound linguini

Mix olive oil, tomatoes, basil, garlic, pepper flakes, salt and pepper. Set aside. Cook pasta in boiling water until al dente, then drain. Pour over uncooked sauce and toss. Season to taste.

SPINACH APPLE SALAD

2 tablespoons unsweetened applesauce
2 tablespoons cider vinegar
1 tablespoon vegetable oil
¼ teaspoon sugar
1 cup diced unpeeled apple

¼ cup chopped onion
¼ cup raisins
2 cups torn fresh spinach
2 cups torn romaine lettuce

In a small bowl combine applesauce, vinegar, oil and sugar; mix well. Add apple onion and raisins. Toss lightly to coat. Cover and let stand for 10 minutes. Just before serving combine spinach and romaine in a large salad bowl, add apple mixture and toss.

STRAWBERRY CLOUD

1 (8 ounce) package strawberry gelatin
2½ cups water

1 (3 ounce) package cook and serve
   vanilla pudding mix
1 (8 ounce) carton frozen light whipped
   topping, thawed

In a saucepan over medium heat, cook and stir gelatin, pudding mix and water until mixture boils, about 15 minutes. Cool until partially set; fold in whipped topping. Spoon into individual dishes. Chill until ready to serve.

IV ~ April ~ Breads and Rolls

Not everything that can be counted counts,
and not everything that counts can be counted.

~ Albert Einstein

APRIL ~ BREADS AND ROLLS

A great addition to any meal, whether it is breakfast, lunch or dinner, is home made-biscuits or bread that is easy to make. The following recipes can be served as a complement to any meal.

QUICK BISCUITS

2 cups flour	**1 teaspoon sugar (optional)**
1 teaspoon salt	**¼ cup mayonnaise**
1 tablespoon baking powder	**1 cup milk**

Preheat oven to 375°. Sift flour, salt and baking powder and sugar. Add mayonnaise to milk and add to flour mixture just until blended. Drop mixture by rounded tablespoons onto a large ungreased baking sheet, 1 inch apart. Bake at 375° for 10 minutes or until biscuits are golden.

LIGHT AS A FEATHER MUFFINS

¼ cup sugar	**½ teaspoon salt**
¼ cup soft shortening	**4 teaspoon baking powder**
1 egg	**1 cup milk**
1¾ cups sifted flour	

Preheat oven to 375 degrees. Mix together sugar and soft shortening. Blend in egg. Sift together flour, salt and baking powder. Stir in alternately with milk. Fill greased muffin cups ⅔ full. Bake until golden brown at 375° for 20 to 25 minutes. Serve hot.

SIX WEEKS MUFFINS

2 cups water	**1 cup shortening, melted**
6 cups All-Bran	**3 cups sugar**
4 eggs	**5 cups flour**
5 teaspoons baking soda	**1 teaspoon salt**
1 cup buttermilk	**raisins if desired**

Preheat oven to 400°. Boil 2 cups water and shortening with 2 cups All-Bran, cool. Beat together sugar and eggs. Sift flour, baking soda and salt. Add this alternately with the buttermilk to the egg and sugar mixture. Add 4 cups All-Bran to first All-Bran mixture. Add flour mixture and blend well. Place mixture in muffin pans as needed. Bake at 400° for 20 minutes or until done when tested. Add raisins if desired. Keep remaining batter in a tightly covered container in the refrigerator. Yields 6-8 dozen muffins. This will keep six weeks.

CORN BREAD

1 cup flour	¾ teaspoon baking soda
1 teaspoon salt	1½ cups corn meal
2 eggs	1½ cups buttermilk
3 tablespoons shortening, melted	

Sift and then measure the flour. Sift again with the baking soda, salt and corn meal. Combine well beaten eggs, buttermilk and melted shortening. Add the liquid ingredients to the dry ingredients stirring only until smooth.

Turn into a well greased 8 or 9 inch pan. Bake in 425° oven 25-20 minutes.

You may make muffins, place batter into greased muffin pans about ⅔ filled. Bake in 425° oven 12-15 minutes.

BANANA NUT BREAD

½ cup butter	1 teaspoon baking soda
1 cup sugar	¼ teaspoon salt
2 eggs well beaten	1 cup sour milk (or buttermilk)
3 medium ripe bananas, mashed	½ cup chopped nuts
2 cups flour	

Preheat oven to 350°. Cream butter and sugar together thoroughly. Add eggs and beat well. Add mashed bananas. Sift flour, baking soda and salt together. Add alternately with sour milk (or buttermilk) to banana mixture. Add nuts and mix. Turn into greased loaf pan and spread evenly. Bake 1 hour or until bread springs back when touched.

PUMPKIN BREAD

1 cup sugar	½ teaspoon salt
½ cup brown sugar, firmly packed	½ teaspoon nutmeg
1 cup cooked or canned pumpkin	½ teaspoon cinnamon
½ cup salad oil	¼ teaspoon ginger
2 eggs (unbeaten)	1 cup raisins
2 cups sifted flour	½ cup chopped nuts
1 teaspoon soda	¼ cup water

Preheat oven to 350°. Combine sugars, pumpkin, oil and eggs; beat until well blended. Sift together flour, soda, salt and spices; add to pumpkin mixture and mix well. Stir in raisins, nuts and water. Spoon into well greased 9x5x3 inch loaf pan. Bake at 350° for 55-65 minutes, or until done when tested. Turn out on rack to cool thoroughly.

IRISH SODA BREAD

4 cups flour
2 teaspoons baking powder
1 teaspoons baking soda
1 teaspoon salt
2 tablespoons sugar

1 cup currants or raisins
1 tablespoon caraway seeds
2 cups buttermilk
1 egg
2-3 tablespoons milk

Preheat oven to 350°. Combine flour, baking powder, soda, salt, sugar, raisins, and caraway seeds. Stir together buttermilk and egg. Add to dry ingredients and mix well. Grease a 10 inch oven proof skillet with vegetable shortening. Add bread dough and dot with pieces of butter. Bake for 45 to 50 minutes at 350°. When done brush with sweet milk, and immediately turn out onto cooling rack. Can use a loaf pan to bake in.

CARROT AND BRAN MUFFINS
"Look for Bran in Health Food Section of Market"

1½ cups unprocessed bran (not cereal)
1 cup whole wheat flour
½ teaspoon salt
½ cup walnuts or almonds
1 egg, slightly beaten
½ cup honey
3 tablespoons salad oil

¼ cup wheat germ
1 teaspoon each baking powder and soda
1 cup shredded carrots
1 cup raisins or chopped dates, figs, or
   prunes
¾ cup milk

In mixing bowl, stir together bran, wheat germ, flour, baking powder, soda, and salt. Add carrots, nuts and dried fruit. Mix to distribute evenly. Make well in center of mixture. Combine egg with milk, honey and oil. Add all at once to flour mixture. Stir to moisten. Spoon into greased or paper lined muffin pan filling about ¾ full. Bake at 400° for 15 to 20 minutes or until done. Serve warm with butter and honey. Makes about 18 muffins.

HONEY BUTTER

Make by whipping together 1 part mild flavored honey and 2 soft parts butter. Store in refrigerator.

NO NEED TO KNEAD BRAN BREAD
"Makes One Nutritious Loaf"

3½ cups flour
1½ teaspoons salt
½ cup honey
2 cups bran cereal or buds,
   or 3 cups bran flakes
1 egg

½ cup instant non-fat dry milk
2 packages active dry yeast
1¼ cups warm water (105-115°)
⅓ cup butter

In large bowl, stir together 3 cups flour, dry milk and salt. Set aside. Combine yeast, honey and warm water in large mixer bowl. Stir in bran cereal. Let stand 2 to 3 minutes or until cereal is softened. Add butter, egg and about half of the flour mixture. Beat at medium speed 2 minutes, scraping sides of bowl occasionally. Stir in remaining flour mixture by hand. Add the remaining ½ cup flour, if necessary, to form stiff sticky dough. Cover. Let rise in warm place, free from draft, until double in size (about 1 hour). Stir down dough. Place in 9x5x3 inch loaf pan greased or sprayed with pan coating. Bake at 375° for 50 minutes or until done. Remove from pan. Brush top of loaf with warm honey to glaze if desired. Serve plain or toasted with butter and honey.

BLUEBERRY MUFFINS

1¾ cups all purpose flour
⅓ cup sugar
2½ teaspoons baking powder
½ teaspoon salt

1 cup fresh or unthawed frozen blueberries
¾ cup milk
1 egg
⅓ cup butter

In a large bowl combine flour, sugar, baking powder and salt. Stir in blueberries.
Add milk, egg and butter. Mix just until dry ingredients are moistened. The batter will be lumpy. Do not over beat. Spoon batter into twelve greased muffin cups.

Bake 375° for 25 minutes or until tops spring back when lightly touched. Serve warm.

V ~ MAY ~ APPETIZERS

Most of all the other beautiful things in life come by twos
and threes, by dozens and hundreds. Plenty of roses,
stars, sunsets, rainbows, brothers and sisters, aunts
and cousins, but only one mother in the world.

~ Kate Douglas Wiggin

MAY ~ APPETIZERS

Every May we set one day aside to honor our mothers. Why should it be just one day? Mothers give so much of their time and love to make sure you learn not only the "A-B-C's", but how important it is to be a caring person and take an active part in the community where you live.

From now on just take the time when least expected, and do something special for your mom, or whoever is responsible for your well being. The recipes in this section are easy to do, and don't take a lot of time. Help may be needed for some tasks, but that is the special time for working together and getting to know someone. Now go find something special to make and enjoy.

Appetizers can be fun to make, and can be either simple or fancy. It is up to the cook how much time and effort you want to take in preparing the appetizers. The following recipes are easy to prepare, but nice to look at and good to eat.

ZUCCHINI APPETIZERS

3 cups zucchini, chopped fine
1 handful parsley, chopped fine
1 onion, chopped fine
1 clove garlic, chopped fine
½ cup salad oil
½ cup grated parmesan or cheddar cheese

½ teaspoon marjoram
½ teaspoon salt
4 eggs slightly beaten
1 cup biscuit mix
salt and pepper to taste

Preheat over to 350°. Combine zucchini, parsley, onion, garlic, oil, cheese, marjoram, seasoned salt, eggs, biscuit mix, salt and pepper. Mix well. Bake in 9x12 inch pan 20 to 25 minutes. Cut into one inch squares. Serve warm or cold. Can be frozen for future use.

GUACAMOLE DIP

1 small chili pepper (or use canned chopped)
1 medium onion
1 small clove garlic
1 small tomato peeled
2 medium ripe avocadoes

1 tablespoon fresh lemon or lime juice
¾ teaspoon salt
pepper to taste
Dash of seasoned salt
Dash of dry mustard

Chop chili pepper, onion, garlic, peeled tomato, and blend. Cut avocadoes into halves; remove seed and skin; mash with chili mixture. Blend in lemon or lime juice, salt, pepper, seasoned salt, and dry mustard. Serve with crackers, corn chips, potato chips, or tortillas. Yields 1½ cups.

SPINACH DIP

1 cup sour cream	1 package dry vegetable soup mix
1 cup mayonnaise	1 box chopped frozen spinach, thawed and drained
5 green onions, chopped fine	1 loaf sourdough French bread

Mix sour cream, mayonnaise, onions, soup mix, and spinach in blender. Hollow out a round loaf of sourdough bread and fill with dip; use bread cubes from the center of loaf to dip.

TANGY EGG SPREAD

4 eggs	1 teaspoon Worcestershire sauce
3 strips crisp bacon (crumbled)	¼ cup mayonnaise
1 teaspoon horseradish	¼ teaspoon salt
1 teaspoon minced onion	

Mix together well hard-cooked eggs, bacon, horseradish, minced onion, Worcestershire sauce, mayonnaise and salt. Makes 1 cup. Serve on crackers.

ONION DIP

1 package onion soup mix	1 pint Sour Cream or Imo

Mix together thoroughly and chill until ready to serve.

RAW VEGETABLE PLATE

Cut any of your favorite vegetables into strips, and arrange them on a plate in an attractive pattern. Vegetable suggestions: carrots, celery, bell peppers, cauliflower, zucchini, turnips, parsnips, or any other raw vegetable you wish.

Any of the above dips are great for dipping vegetables.

STUFFED EGGS

6 hard cooked eggs
2 teaspoons prepared mustard
½ teaspoon Worcestershire Sauce
Parsley & paprika

2 tablespoons mayonnaise (more if needed)
½ teaspoon A-1 Sauce
salt & pepper to taste

Hard cook the eggs by placing the eggs in a pan with cold water. Bring the water to a boil and then turn off the heat. Let the eggs stay in the hot water for 15 minutes, then drain off the water and pour cold water over the eggs. Drain the water off, and then shake the pan gently to crack the eggs for easy pealing. Set the eggs aside to cool before removing the shells. Cut the egg in half lengthwise and remove the yolk and place it in a small dish, mash the egg yolk and remaining ingredients mix well with a fork until smooth. After the mixture is thoroughly mixed, using a spoon, fill the center of each half egg. Garnish with parsley & paprika if desired.

EGGS WITH VEGGIES

4 hard cooked eggs
2 tablespoons plain yogurt
2 tablespoons finely chopped zucchini
1 tablespoon finely chopped celery
Prepare as you would stuffed eggs.

1 teaspoon chopped fresh dill or
 ¼ teaspoon dried dill
¼ teaspoon prepared mustard
⅛ teaspoon pepper

FRESH FRUIT

Pineapple
Watermelon
Bananas

Strawberries
Cantaloupe

After slicing the bananas dip, the slices in the pineapple juice, or small bowl of water with lemon juice. This prevents them from browning.

With a melon baller make melon balls from whatever melon or melons your have chosen. Place the fruit attractively on a plate, or mounded in bowls. Serve with toothpicks.

PINEAPPLE DIP

1 (8 ounce) package cream cheese, softened
1 cup plain yogurt
2 tablespoons honey

2 teaspoons crushed gingerroot
1 (8 ounce) can crushed pineapple, drained

Beat cream cheese, yogurt, honey and gingerroot in medium bowl until creamy. Fold in pineapple. Cover and refrigerate at least 1 hour or until chilled. Use as a dip for your favorite fruits.

STUFFED CELERY

Celery

any of the suggested fillings

Celery is really great when cut into 1½" lengths and then filled with whatever you like. Peanut butter, any of the cheeses in jars: pimento, pineapple, etc., or use cream cheese. If cream cheese is used let it stand at room temperature until it is soft. Then mix 3 ounces cream cheese with 1 teaspoon Worcestershire Sauce, 1 teaspoon A1 Sauce, and 1 tablespoon mayonnaise.

Another great mix is:
1 (6 ounce) container pineapple yogurt
½ cup small curd cottage cheese
½ cup chopped walnuts

Mix and stuff the celery as directed.

RELISH PLATE

Black olives, Green olives, or any of your favorite pickles cut into small pieces, and a jar of marinated vegetables.

Arrange the above foods attractively on a plate. You may add any of your favorite vegetables.

CHEESE APPLE PLATE

Pick a variety of your favorite cheeses and crisp apples. Slice the apples into a small bowl that has fresh lemon squeezed into a small amount of water. Add red or green grapes, fresh strawberries, fresh apricots, or any other fresh fruit that you think might be good. Arrange fruit on a platter. This is a good appetizer or may be used as a dessert.

Suggested cheeses: provolone, Swiss, any cheddar, colby, mozzarella, or any other that can be cut into serving pieces.

VI ~ June ~ Father's Day
~ Main Dish ~ Vegetables

No man can possibly know what life means.
    What the world means, what anything means,
    Until he has a child and loves it. And then the
    Whole universe changes and nothing will ever
    Again seem exactly as it seemed before.

~ Lafcadio Hearn - From: My Father

When first thinking about a cookbook, I had a definite purpose for writing a book that would encourage families to work together in the kitchen. It would be a book that had some easy recipes for younger family members, and additional recipes for any members of the family that have an interest in being creative in the kitchen.

Father's Day is in June, and this is a special day to honor fathers. What better way to bring the family together and to have memories to share than to plan a special family breakfast, brunch, picnic, or dinner and use this time to prepare something for that special father. Working together would be a great experience that would have a very special meaning to all who participate, and then a great sharing time with dad and the entire family.

HEARTY SAUSAGE CASSEROLE

1½ pounds bulk pork sausage
1 small clove garlic, minced
⅓ cup chopped onion
3 tablespoons flour

1 teaspoon oregano
⅛ teaspoon pepper
1 (16 ounce can) tomatoes, undrained
2 cups cooked mixed vegetables, drained

TOPPING:

1 egg slightly beaten
1 cup shredded cheddar cheese
⅔ cup milk

1 cup pancake mix
½ teaspoon dry mustard
1 tablespoon cooking oil

Preheat oven to 350°

Brown sausage, garlic and onion; drain fat. Stir in flour and seasonings. Add tomatoes and vegetables; cook, stirring constantly, until thickened. Simmer while preparing topping. Lightly spoon pancake mix into measuring cup, level off. In medium bowl, combine all topping ingredients except ½ cup cheese, blend well.

Pour hot meat mixture into shallow 2 quart casserole or 12x8 inch baking dish. Spoon topping over meat, sprinkle with reserved cheese. Bake uncovered 20-25 minutes until golden brown. Serve immediately.

SKILLET DINNER

1 (10 ounce) package refrigerated biscuits
½ cup shredded cheddar cheese
1 pound ground meat
1 cup shredded Swiss or cheddar cheese

3 ounce package cream cheese softened
3 tablespoons dry onion soup mix
1 can cream of mushroom soup
2 eggs, beaten

Preheat oven to 375°. Separate biscuit dough into 10 biscuits; press or roll each to a 4 inch circle. Combine cream cheese, shredded cheddar cheese and 1 tablespoon of the dry onion soup mix; blend well. Spoon about one tablespoon cream cheese mixture onto center of each biscuit. Fold dough in half over filling; press edges with fork to seal.

In 10 inch fry pan, brown meat with remaining 2 tablespoons of the dry onion soup mix, drain. Stir in soup, 1 cup Swiss cheese and eggs; heat until hot and bubbly. Transfer meat mixture to a 12x8 inch baking dish; arrange filled biscuits on hot meat mixture. Bake 22-28 minutes until deep golden brown. Serve immediately.

PARMESAN NOODLES

1 package broad egg noodles
¼ cup margarine
2 tablespoons finely chopped fresh parsley

2 cups corn flakes, crushed to ½ cup
1 cup grated parmesan cheese

In large saucepan cook noodles according to package directions. Drain thoroughly do not rinse. In same saucepan, combine drained hot noodles with margarine and parsley. Add cereal mixed with parmesan cheese, toss lightly. Serve immediately on warm platter.

FISH FILLETS SMOTHERED WITH RICE AND MUSHROOMS

1 large onion
2 cups fresh sliced mushrooms
1 stalk celery, diced
1 clove garlic finely minced
4 teaspoons butter
pinch of sage
salt and pepper to taste

2 cups cooked rice
1 pound fish fillets
3 tablespoons sour cream
1 can cream of mushroom soup
parsley for garnish
sliced lemon wedges

Sauté vegetables lightly in butter or margarine. Add seasoning. Mix cooked vegetables with cooked rice. Layer the mixture in between the fillets. Mix sour cream and soup together and spread over the top. Bake at 375° for 30 to 40 minutes. Serve with parsley and sliced lemon wedges.

PARMESAN ZUCCHINI FRITTATS

5 tablespoons butter
¼ cup chopped onion
½ teaspoon oregano leaves
3 small zucchini, sliced thinly
1 teaspoon salt, divided

2 eggs, slightly beaten
1½ cups milk
½ cup parmesan cheese
½ cup buttermilk baking mix

Grease baking dish. In skillet sauté onions, oregano, zucchini and ½ teaspoon salt until zucchini is tender but crisp. Blend eggs, milk, cheese, baking mix, 2 tablespoons butter and ½ teaspoon salt. Pour into baking dish, spoon zucchini over the top. Bake in 375° 30-40 minutes.

GARDEN CASSEROLE

1½ cups cottage cheese
½ cup sour cream
1 tablespoon flour
3 eggs
2 tablespoons minced onion

¼ teaspoon pepper
2 (10 ounce) packages chopped broccoli,
    cooked and drained
1 (17 ounce) can whole kernel corn, drained
¼ cup grated parmesan cheese
salt to taste

Blend the cottage cheese, sour cream, flour, eggs, and seasonings together, fold in vegetables. Pour into 2 quart casserole, top with parmesan cheese. Bake at 325° 45 minutes.

RICE AND BEANS WITH SAUSAGE

½ pound hot or sweet Italian sausage
    cut into ¼ inch slices
1 large onion sliced
1 medium green pepper, halved,
    seeded and diced
1 medium red pepper halved and diced
1 clove garlic minced
1 medium tomato chopped

1½ teaspoons salt
½ teaspoon leaf oregano crumbled
¼ teaspoon liquid red pepper
2 cups water
2 cups Minute Rice
1 can black beans, drained

Cook sausage in a large skillet over moderate heat until browned on both sides. Remove with slotted spoon to paper towel. Keep warm.

Sauté onion, green and red peppers and garlic in fat remaining in skillet until tender. Add tomato, salt, oregano, liquid red pepper and water.

Bring to a boil, stir in rice and beans. Remove from heat, cover and let stand 8 minutes or until liquid is absorbed. Fluff up rice.

Spoon mixture onto serving plate and arrange sausage on top.

MUSHROOM CASSEROLE

1 pound mushrooms, sliced	½ cup mayonnaise
1 cup chopped celery	salt and pepper to taste
¼ cup chopped onion	2 eggs
½ cup chopped green pepper	1½ cups milk
3 tablespoons butter	1 can mushroom soup
8 slices bread	grated cheese

Sauté vegetables in butter. Butter 3 slices bread and cut into 1" squares. Put bread on the bottom of buttered casserole. Combine the vegetable mixture with mayonnaise, salt & pepper. Put mixture into casserole, top with 3 more slices of bread cut into cubes.

Pour egg and milk mixture over casserole. May refrigerate at this point. One hour before serving spoon mushroom soup over the casserole and the remaining 2 slices of bread which have been diced fine. Cover and bake at 300° for 60 minutes. Sprinkle grated cheese over top and bake 10 minutes uncovered.

BEEF WITH APPLES

4 Granny Smith apples	⅛ teaspoon cinnamon
2 tablespoons butter	Small amount of beef broth if needed
2 tablespoons light brown sugar	⅓ cup golden raisins
1 tablespoon lemon juice	6 large slices leftover cooked beef
1 teaspoon nutmeg	(boiled or roasted)
	4 cups hot cooked rice

Core apples; do not peel; cut crosswise into thick slices. Fry in butter until lightly browned. Combine lemon juice, nutmeg and cinnamon; add to apples; simmer until apples are tender. Add small amount of beef broth if needed. Stir in raisins. Add beef slices; simmer until meat is heated through. Serve on rice.

CREAMY ZUCCHINI

4 medium zucchini trimmed and grated	Sour Cream
Salt	Pinch dried or ½ teaspoon fresh oregano
Butter	

Remove and discard ends from zucchini; grate into a bowl. Sprinkle lightly with salt and let sit for 10 minutes; squeeze dry in a towel. Melt butter in a heavy saucepan, put in zucchini and simmer for a few minutes until any liquid has evaporated. Add a little sour cream and the oregano and serve immediately.

RED SNAPPER

2 cups diced pineapple
2 cups diced seedless cucumber
2 cups diced plum tomatoes
1 cup peeled diced red onion
¼ cup pineapple juice
1 tablespoon minced garlic
2 teaspoons fresh minced ginger

1 teaspoon cornstarch
salt to taste
½ pound red snapper
1 teaspoon olive oil
1 teaspoon lime juice
2 teaspoons fresh basil

Prepare the salsa. In a heavy saucepan combine the diced pineapple, cucumber, tomatoes and onion, plus pineapple juice. Simmer over medium-high heat, stirring occasionally for 5 minutes. Reduce heat to medium and add garlic and ginger; cook stirring for 5 minutes. Remove ¼ cup of the liquid from the saucepan to a small bowl. Add the cornstarch and stir until smooth. Stir the mixture back into the simmering salsa and cook, stirring for about 2 minutes or until slightly thickened. Season with salt. Set aside. Place the fish, skin side down on a foil lined boiler pan. Brush fish with olive oil and drizzle with lime juice. Sprinkle with salt and pepper. Broil 3 inches from heat for 7 minutes or until the fish is cooked through and flakes easily when tested with a fork. Meanwhile, reheat salsa and stir in basil. Serve the fish over rice in a shallow bowls: spoon the salsa over the fish.

BROILED SALMON

1 pound salmon fillet
1 lemon

2 tablespoons stone ground mustard
1 tablespoon chopped fresh dill or ¾ teaspoon dried

Preheat broiler. Set oven rack 3-4 inches from the element. Rinse fish, pat dry, and lay skin side down on a baking sheet sprayed with Pam. With a zester or grater remove zest (yellow part of peel only) from lemon; squeeze 1 tablespoon juice from lemon. Mix lemon zest, lemon juice, mustard and dill. Brush mixture over salmon. Broil salmon until opaque, about 5-6 minutes for ½ inch thick fillet, 10 to 12 minutes for 1 inch fillet.

CHILI CHICKEN

1 egg
½ cup tomato juice
1 tablespoon oil

¼ cup flour
1 envelope chili seasoning mix
1 frying chicken, cut up (or favorite parts)

Lightly beat together egg, tomato juice, and oil in medium size bowl. Add flour and contents of chili seasoning. Stir just until blended. Dip chicken pieces in mixture, turning to coat completely. Place in a greased shallow baking pan skin side up if you do not skin the chicken. Bake in 400° oven 50 to 60 minutes or until chicken is tender.

STUFFED CHARD

1 pound ground beef	parsley
1 onion, chopped finely	Swiss chard, large leaves
garlic, salt and pepper to taste	juice of ½ lemon
¾ cup uncooked rice	Water
1 small can tomato sauce	

Combine the above ingredients, except for the chard, water and lemon. Set aside.

Cut out white center of Swiss chard and cut large leaves in half down the center. Bring to boil (green part) and take off range immediately. Leaves will be limp and pliable. Put about ¼ cup of the mixture you have set aside on each leaf and roll. Put in tightly covered pan with water and juice of a half a lemon. Simmer about ½ hour until rice is cooked.

A good way to use the white portion of Swiss chard is to fry an onion in oil with chopped Swiss chard, add crumbs from 2 slices of fresh bread, 1 egg, 1 cup milk, salt and pepper to taste. Put in greased baking dish and bake covered about ½ hour in 350° oven until chard is tender.

TUNA CASSEROLE

1 (6 ounce) package medium noodles cooked	1 teaspoon salt
1 (12 ounce) can tuna	1 can cream of celery soup
½ cup mayonnaise	½ cup milk
1 cup celery	1 cup shredded sharp cheese
⅓ cup onion	½ cup slivered almonds
¼ cup green pepper	

Preheat oven to 375°
Combine noodles, tuna, mayonnaise, celery, onions, green pepper and salt. Heat soup and milk then add with cheese to the tuna mix. Put in a casserole and top with almonds. Bake 45 minutes.

MEAT LOAF

8 dark green cabbage leaves	1 cup soft bread crumbs
½ cup instant nonfat dry milk	½ cup water
½ teaspoon salt	¼ teaspoon pepper
1 pound ground round	1 cup shredded cheddar cheese, divided

SAUCE

½ cup chopped onion | 1 diced tomato
½ cup chopped celery | 1 teaspoon Italian seasoning
2 tablespoons butter

For sauce sauté onion and celery in butter in heavy saucepan until tender, about 5 minutes. Remove from heat and stir in diced tomato and Italian seasoning. Bring to a boil, stirring frequently. Simmer 15 minutes, uncovered. Set aside. Preheat oven to 325°.

For meatloaf, chop cabbage coarsely. Cook in salted boiling water uncovered for 5 minutes. Set aside.

Combine bread crumbs, dry milk, water, salt and pepper in a large mixing bowl. Mix in meat. Pat half of meat mixture into bottom of an 8 inch square baking pan. Combine cabbage, and half of the cheese. Spread over meat. Top with remaining meat mixture. Spoon sauce over all. Bake 55 to 60 minutes. Remove from oven sprinkle with remaining cheese. Wait 10 minutes before serving.

BAKED FLOUNDER AND VEGETABLES

1 medium onion, thinly sliced | ¼ cup butter
2 small yellow squash, thinly sliced | 1 pound flounder
1 medium zucchini, cut in julienne strips
½ teaspoon each lemon pepper, dill weed, onion powder
salt to taste

Preheat oven to 400°. Tear off four 12x 8 inch sheets of foil. Place onion and yellow squash and zucchini slices on lower half of each sheet of foil. Combine lemon pepper, dill weed and onion powder; sprinkle half of seasoning mixture over squash and onions. Season with salt. Dot with butter. Layer fish over vegetables then season with salt. Place zucchini strips over fish. Sprinkle with remaining seasoning mixture. Dot with remaining butter. Envelope wrap the foil. Arrange foil packets on baking sheet. Cook 18 to 20 minutes or until envelope puffs. To serve cut "x" in top of packet; fold foil back.

ADAPT YOUR RECIPE: Combine boneless chicken breasts or fish fillets with you choice of julienne vegetables. You may use 1 teaspoon fresh lemon and 1 tablespoon finely chopped onion if you choose.

**6 whole chicken breasts,
  boned, skinned and split**
6 tablespoons butter
1 medium onion, chopped
1 clove garlic, minced
**2 medium apples, cored and
  finely chopped**
1 cup soft bread crumbs

½ teaspoon each crushed rosemary and basil
1 teaspoon salt
flour as needed
¼ cup apple juice
3 tablespoons honey

Place chicken breasts between sheets of waxed paper and pound with mallet until thin. Melt 3 tablespoons of butter in large skillet. Sauté onion and garlic until translucent. Stir in apples, breadcrumbs and seasonings, mixing thoroughly over low heat. Spoon about 3 tablespoons apple mixture onto each breast. Roll up, tucking in ends and secure with wooden picks. Roll in flour. Heat remaining 3 tablespoons butter in skillet and brown rolls well on all sides. Add apple juice and honey. Simmer covered for 25 to 30 minutes. Remove chicken from skillet. Over high heat, boil juices until slightly thickened. Spoon over breasts to glaze. Makes 12 servings.

VII ~ July ~ Summer
~ Ice Cream and Bar-B-Ques

STRAWBERRY FLAVORED DREAM
Collect the dreams you dream today
And hold them in an ice cream cone
Taste them share them with a friend
They taste good
Taste all you can experience
The colors come alive inside you
The flavor takes root inside you
And when the delicious taste begins to fade away...
Buy yourself another ice cream cone...

~ Judith Howard Noyes

JULY ~ SUMMER ~ ICE CREAM AND BAR-B-QUES

Now that summer is here, we can enjoy barbeques and picnics in the park, by a lake, or any of your favorite places. Whether you settle for your own backyard, or hop in the car for a drive, being outside with your family and friends is a great way to spend an afternoon or evening.

When planning a menu for an outdoor activity there is so much to choose from, and you can make it quite simple - that's what I go for - or you can go all out and make it as luxurious as you like. Whatever you decide to do, be sure that anything that you take to eat can be safely stored and eaten without the use of a refrigerator.

ICE CREAM

STRAWBERRY SOUR CREAM ICE CREAM

2 (10 ounce) packages frozen strawberries thawed and drained**
2 cups granulated sugar
4 cups sour cream***

Mix together thawed strawberries, sugar, and sour cream.
Churn freeze.

** I prefer to blend the strawberries in a blender before adding to the rest of the ingredients. This makes a smoother ice cream.
*** You may substitute either Imo or plain yogurt

VANILLA ICE CREAM

1 cup granulated sugar   **⅛ teaspoon salt**
5 cups light cream   **¼ teaspoon vanilla extract**

Combine sugar, cream, vanilla and salt.
Churn freeze.

Using the basic Vanilla Ice Cream you can make a lot of different flavors. These are just a few examples: Peppermint (use crushed hard mints), peach (use fresh peaches), pineapple (use can of crushed pineapple, drained). For other flavors use your imagination.

ICE CREAM TOPPINGS:
SERVE THESE OVER YOUR FAVORITE ICE CREAM
PLUM SAUCE

1½ pounds fresh plums (about 9 medium) quartered
1 to 1½ cups sugar (depending on tartness of plums)
⅛ to ¼ teaspoon cinnamon or nutmeg

1 tablespoon lemon juice
1 cup whipping cream

Stir plums and sugar in heavy saucepan over low heat until juices flow. Bring to boil, stirring, then simmer 3 to 5 minutes or just until plums are tender but still hold there shape. With a slotted spoon, remove plums to bowl. Add remaining ingredients to syrup in pan.

Cook gently over medium heat about 6 minutes or until syrupy. Pour over plums. Chill.

Fold plums into whipped cream. Use as topping or freeze for a quick ice cream.

BASIC SAUCE FOR FRUIT TOPPINGS

⅔ cup evaporated milk
1 cup sugar

1 tablespoon butter
⅛ teaspoon salt

Place the ingredients into a blender. Cover and blend until creamy.

FRESH STRAWBERRY

 Add ½ pint strawberries and 1 thin slice peeled lemon to the basic sauce before blending. When creamy, add another ½ pint strawberries and blend just long enough to cut them up.

BANANA NUT

Add 1 ripe banana, 1 thin slice unpeeled lemon and ½ cup pecans to basic sauce. Cover and run the blender just long enough to coarsely chop the nuts.

FRESH PINEAPPLE

Add 2 cups peeled and cubed fresh pineapple to basic recipe before blending. Cover and blend until finely chopped.

BAR-B-QUES

SOY GRILLED FISH

2 pounds fish fillets cut into serving pieces
¼ teaspoon salt
¼ teaspoon pepper
4 teaspoons soy sauce

4 tablespoons vegetable oil
4 tablespoons lemon juice
4 tablespoons minced parsley

Season fish with salt and pepper. Place on oiled grill or in oiled wire grill basket, or spray foil with nonstick spray. Combine soy sauce, and oil. Grill until golden brown, basting frequently with soy mixture, 5-8 minutes per side. Remove fish to warm platter and keep warm. Add lemon juice and parsley to any remaining soy mixture, heat and pour over fish.

CHEDDAR CHEESE AND ZUCCHINI

6 medium zucchini, scrubbed and ends removed
1 cup shredded sharp cheddar cheese
⅓ cup diced red pepper

⅓ cup diced green pepper
Salt and freshly ground pepper to taste
2 tablespoons butter or margarine

Cut six 12 inch squares of heavy duty aluminum foil. Cut zucchini into ¼ inch slices and place on foil. Mix the cheese, red and green peppers, and divide into six portions. Place one portion on each zucchini. Then add the salt and pepper and dot with butter. Close packages by folding in sides then rolling up ends. Grill about 20 minutes over medium hot coals, turning occasionally.

BRATWURST WITH SAUERKRAUT

6 bratwurst
2 cups sauerkraut, washed and drained
2 tablespoons brown sugar

1 teaspoon caraway seeds
6 frankfurter buns
Dijon or spicy mustard

Split bratwurst lengthwise almost all the way through. Score along edges to keep from curling. Grill about 5 minutes on each side. Heat sauerkraut with brown sugar and caraway seeds until sugar melts and sauerkraut is heated through. Grill split buns just enough to warm and spread with mustard. Place a bratwurst in each one and top with sauerkraut.

BBQ SAUCES

TOMATO MUSTARD SAUCE

2 tablespoons butter
1 stalk celery
2 green onions
2 tablespoons flour

1 teaspoon salt
⅛ teaspoon pepper
1¾ cups canned tomatoes
2 tablespoons prepared mustard

Put all ingredients into blender and blend thoroughly until the vegetables are finely chopped. Pour into saucepan and simmer about 5 minutes. Spoon desired amount on hamburger patty or spread generously on hotdogs.

LEMON PARSLEY SAUCE

½ cup fresh parsley
1 medium onion quartered

1 lemon, peeled, seeded and quartered
½ teaspoon salt

Put all ingredients into blender and blend until smooth. Brush on fish while barbecuing.

BLEU CHEESE BASTING SAUCE

1 cup salad oil
1 cup lemon juice
½ cup bleu cheese

2 tablespoons Worcestershire sauce
1 teaspoon salt
¼ teaspoon pepper

Put all ingredients into blender and blend until smooth.
This is an excellent sauce for turkey or chicken.

LEMON BARBECUE SAUCE

1 glove garlic
½ teaspoon salt
¼ cup salad oil
2 tablespoons chili sauce

½ lemon, seeded and quartered
medium slice of onion
pepper

Put all ingredients into blender and blend until smooth. Brush on chicken or burgers while barbecuing.

SAUCE FOR HOT DOGS

1 pound ground beef
1 (6 ounce) can tomato paste
frankfurters

1 envelope chili seasoning mix
1½ cups water
frankfurter buns

Brown ground beef in skillet, crumbling beef into small pieces. Drain off excess fat. Add contents of chili seasoning, tomato paste and water. Bring to a boil, reduce heat and simmer for 5 minutes. Meanwhile, grill frankfurters. Place hot dogs in buns and spoon sauce over franks. Enough sauce for 10 to 15 frankfurters.

CRANBERRY GLAZE FOR BBQ CHICKEN

1 can jellied cranberry sauce
½ cup packed brown sugar
1 teaspoon dry mustard
1 clove garlic, crushed

¼ cup soy sauce
1 teaspoon salt
1 teaspoon ground ginger
2 tablespoons lemon juice

Combine all ingredients and stir over low heat until melted and smooth. Let stand at room temperature 1 hour. Makes about 1½ cups glaze or enough for 2 chickens. To use, season chicken pieces with salt and pepper and cook on barbecue grill or in oven. During last 20 minutes of cooking, brush several times with glaze.

WHOLE WHEAT BREAD MIX

4 cups all purpose flour
½ cup nonfat dry milk powder
8 teaspoons baking powder
1 cup solid vegetable shortening

1 cup whole wheat flour
3 tablespoons granulated sugar
1 teaspoon salt

In a large mixing bowl mix all purpose flour, whole wheat flour, powdered milk, sugar, baking powder and salt. Stir dry ingredients with a spoon until they are well combined. Add shortening to dry ingredients in mixing bowl. With a pastry blender or a knife cut shortening into dry ingredients. Keep cutting, or use the tips of your fingers to gently mix until the mixture is in fine crumbs. Press with quick light motions, don't overwork mixture. Put mixture into a container and use as needed. This is to be used when you want bread on a camping trip. The mix will keep at room temperature for about one month.

TO COOK BREAD YOU WILL NEED

Long sturdy green twigs that are at least ½ inch thick

A little vegetable oil	**1 paper towel or napkin**
Whole wheat bread mix	**1 large zip lock bag**
3 to 4 tablespoons water for each cup of mix.	**Butter, honey, or jelly**

(You can make 3 rolls from each cup of mix. Be sure to mix well.)

Put twig on a flat surface and with a sharp knife scrape any loose bark from bottom 6 inches of each twig. Set twigs aside***

Put baking mix in the zip lock bag. Use 1 cup mix for every 3 rolls you want to make. Add enough water to the bag to make a stiff dough (you will need 3 to 4 tablespoons water for every cup mix.) Seal the bag and knead bag until dough is well blended.

Divide dough into small portions (3 portions for each cup mix used.) Dip napkin in oil and rub on the scraped end of a twig. Slightly flatten each portion of dough and wrap it around the oiled twig. Keep pressing the dough until it forms a ¼ inch layer completely around twig. Put only one portion of dough on each twig. To cook bread, hold twig so that dough is over glowing coals. Keep turning the twig to cook bread evenly. Cook bread until it is golden brown.

Slip hot bread off twig***. Eat bread with butter and honey or jelly, if desired.

***IT IS BEST TO HAVE AN ADULT HELP
    WITH THE STEPS IN THIS PROCESS.

Twigs come from branches of trees that are on the ground. Do not take branches from trees; use only those found on the ground.

VIII ~ August
~ Refreshing Cool Drinks

Always do right- this will gratify some and astonish the rest.

~ Mark Twain

AUGUST ~ REFRESHING COOL DRINKS

August is a month for patio entertaining and sitting outdoors when it is hot and your thoughts are how to keep cool. Now that summer is here in all its splendor, it is time to enjoy those lazy summer afternoons and evenings just relaxing with the family and friends enjoying the outdoors as much as possible. One way to enjoy a lazy summer afternoon or evening is to serve a punch or some type of cool drink with a tray of cookies or whatever light snack you might prefer. Just pick one of the recipes in this chapter and you and your family can just sit back relax and enjoy a time of fellowship with your friends.

TOMATO JUICE

4 cups tomato juice
2 teaspoons prepared horseradish
salt to taste

¼ cup lemon juice
1 teaspoon Worcestershire sauce

Mix together and chill before serving. Serve over ice.

STRAWBERRY ~ APPLE FLOAT

1 10 ounce package frozen sliced strawberries, thawed
1 cup nonfat milk
1 scoop vanilla ice cream

1¼ cup apple juice
1 cup carbonated water

Mix in blender and serve

STRAWBERRY ~ PEACH FIZZ

1½ cups chilled strawberry flavored carbonated beverage
Peach flavor yogurt (about 2 cups)

Place the ingredients in a blender. Cover and blend on high speed about 10 seconds or until smooth. Serve immediately over ice. 4 servings.

FRUIT SHAKE

1 container (16 ounces) fat free or plain vanilla yogurt (about 2 cups)
1 package (10 ounces) frozen strawberries or raspberries, partially thawed
1 medium banana, sliced (about 1 cup)

Place all ingredients in a blender. Cover and blend on high speed about 30 seconds or until smooth. 4 servings.

ORANGE MILK COOLER

1 (6 ounce) can frozen orange juice concentrate   **2½ cups milk**

Combine all ingredients in blender. Mix until fluffy. Makes about 5 cups.

FROSTY MEAL

1 cup strawberries
1 cup milk
2 teaspoons sugar

½ banana
2½ teaspoons vanilla extract
2 ice cubes, cracked

Remove hulls from berries. Combine all ingredients in electric blender. Whir until smooth and fluffy. Makes about 2 cups.

CUCUMBER ~ YOGURT

1 cup plain yogurt
1 medium cucumber, skin and seeds removed
½ teaspoon salt
2 cubes ice, crushed

1½ cups milk
½ cup sliced green onions
½ teaspoon dried mint leaves

Whir in electric blender until smooth and blended.

BANANA CHOCOLATE FROSTY

1 cup cold milk
1 scoop chocolate ice cream

1 ripe banana, mashed

Blend all ingredients in blender. Makes 1 serving. Top with scoop of ice cream, if desired.

BOYSENBERRY FLIP

1 cup milk   **1 (8 ounce) carton of boysenberry yogurt**

Blend until smooth in blender. Makes 2 cups.

CRANBERRY ~ LEMON SHAKE

2 cups water
½ cup instant nonfat dry milk
1 pint lemon sherbet softened

¾ cup (half of a 12 ounce can) frozen
cranberry juice concentrate, thawed
Lemon sherbet

Place water, concentrate and dry milk in blender, cover and blend until well combined. Add softened sherbet and blend until smooth. Serve immediately in a tall chilled glasses garnished with a small scoop of lemon sherbet.

IX ~ September
~ Breakfast and Lunch

Opportunities multiply as they are seized.

~ Sun Tzu

SEPTEMBER ~ BREAKFAST AND LUNCH

September is the month when summer is winding down and school is about to start. The summer has been one of creating memories, trips, family barbecues, picnics, and just enjoying the outdoors as much as possible. Now it is time to again come back to some kind of schedule in daily activities. For students it is a time to see old friends and meet new ones, finding out what the new teacher is like, and returning to a routine of early rising to be on time for school.

For parents it is having to tell students: "Rise and shine or you will be late," making sure lunches are ready or lunch money is available, and checking to see if all school assignments are completed. This time can be either hectic, or it can be a time to work together and make sure all tasks are completed. It is up to all members of the family to make the early morning tasks run smoothly so that everyone has a wonderful start to a new day.

APPLE MUFFINS

Apple muffins are great for breakfast, the lunch bag or snacks.

1 cup grated apple	**¼ cup sugar**
¼ cup salad oil	**½ teaspoon salt**
1 egg	**½ teaspoon cinnamon**
1 cup milk	**3 teaspoons baking powder**
2 cups flour	

Stir together apples, oil, egg and milk. Mix with all remaining ingredients and spoon into greased muffin tin. Bake at 375° for 18-20 minutes, or until done.

FRESH PUMPKIN MUFFINS

2 cups sifted flour	**¼ cup sugar**
3 teaspoons baking powder	**½ teaspoon salt**
½ teaspoon cinnamon	**1 egg**
½ cup milk	**1 cup mashed cooked fresh pumpkin**
¼ cup salad oil	

Sift flour, sugar, baking powder, salt and cinnamon into a bowl. Set aside. Beat egg. Mix in milk, pumpkin and salad oil. Make a well in center of flour mixture; pour in pumpkin mixture all at once. Stir quickly until flour is just moistened. Fill greased muffin cups ⅔ full.

Bake in 375° oven 25 minutes or until done. Run spatula around each muffin to loosen.

FRESH PUMPKIN

Using a fresh pumpkin cut it into sections that will fit in a steamer pan. Steam until pumpkin is soft; scoop the pumpkin out after it has cooled. This can be used in recipes instead of canned pumpkin.

PEACH STREUSEL COFFEE CAKE

CAKE INGREDIENTS

½ cup butter, softened
2 eggs
2 cups flour
1 teaspoon baking soda
1 cup sour cream

1 cup sugar
1 teaspoon vanilla
1 teaspoon baking powder
¼ teaspoon salt

TOPPING

½ cup flour
½ cup sugar
¼ teaspoon nutmeg
1 (16 ounce) can sliced peaches,
   drained and sliced

¼ cup butter
½ teaspoon cinnamon
½ cup chopped pecans or other nuts

Preheat oven to 350°. Grease two round cake pans. Cream butter with sugar until light and fluffy. Add eggs, one at a time, beating well after each addition. Blend in vanilla. Combine flour, baking powder, soda, and salt then add to creamed mixture alternately with sour cream. To make topping, combine flour, butter, sugar, cinnamon, nutmeg, and nuts. Spread ¼ of batter in each prepared pan, and top with ¼ of topping mixture. Spoon remaining batter over topping and spread evenly; sprinkle half of peaches over each cake. Sprinkle with remaining topping. Bake 35-40 minutes. Cool.

BUTTERMILK PANCAKES

2 cups flour
1 teaspoon baking soda
1 teaspoon salt
1 tablespoon sugar

1 egg
2 ¼ cups buttermilk
1 tablespoon butter melted

Sift flour with baking soda, salt and sugar. Combine well beaten egg, milk and melted shortening. Add the liquid ingredients to the dry ingredients, stirring only until smooth. Heat griddle slowly and evenly. Pour batter onto griddle using a ¼ or ⅓ measuring cup, depending on size of pancakes. Bake, turning each pancake when it is browned on the underside, and puffed and slightly set on top. Turn only once. Serve immediately on warm plate.

ORANGE RAISIN SQUARES

2 cups flour
1 teaspoon baking soda
¼ teaspoon salt
½ teaspoon ground nutmeg
1 teaspoon ground cinnamon
½ cup butter
1½ cups firmly packed brown sugar

2 eggs beaten
2 tablespoon orange juice
1 cup raisins
1 cup chopped nuts
1 teaspoon grated orange peel
powdered sugar

Preheat over to 325°. Lightly grease 9X12 inch pan. Stir together flour, soda, salt and spices, set aside. Cream butter and brown sugar. Add eggs and orange juice, beating until fluffy. Gradually add dry ingredients, mixing well. Fold in raisins, nuts, and orange peel. Spread evenly into prepared pan. Bake 35 to 40 minutes or until toothpick inserted in center comes out clean and squares begin to pull away from sides of pan. Cool on rack. Cut into squares. Sprinkle with powdered sugar if desired.

CHILI ~ STEAK SANDWICHES

4-6 cube steaks
1 envelope chili seasoning mix
2 cups tomato juice
¼ cup butter or margarine softened

¼ cup grated parmesan cheese
6 hard rolls, split
1 green pepper
1 tablespoon oil or shortening

Cut cube steaks into 1 inch cubes, Brown in oil in a large skillet. Add contents of seasoning mix envelope and tomato juice, simmer 10 minutes, stirring occasionally. Combine butter and cheese; spread on rolls. Spoon steak and sauce into rolls and top with thinly sliced green pepper.

BREAKFAST KABOBS

1⅓ cups cubed fresh pineapple
1 cup strawberries
1 cup strawberry or pineapple yogurt
2 tablespoons honey

1 papaya, pared and cubed
1 banana, peeled and sliced
¼ cup flaked coconut
1 tablespoon lime juice

Using ten six inch skewers, alternately thread pineapple, papaya, strawberries, and banana. Combine yogurt, coconut, honey and lime juice; serve with kabobs.

WHITE BREAD

1 cup milk
3 tablespoons sugar
1 tablespoon salt
2 tablespoons shortening

1 cup lukewarm water
2 packages dry yeast
4½ cups unsifted flour

Scald milk then stir in sugar, salt and shortening. Cool to lukewarm. Measure warm water into large warm bowl. Put in yeast stir until dissolved. Add lukewarm milk mixture. Stir in flour, beat 2 minutes. Cover let rise until doubled, about 60 minutes.

On a floured board knead dough down, kneading for 7 minutes. Put into two greased loaf pans. Let rise again. Bake at 375° for 60 minutes. Remove from pan, cool on rack. Slice and enjoy.

CHICKEN ALMOND SPREAD FOR SANDWICH

1 cup chopped chicken, cooked
¼ cup chopped raisins
½ cup mayonnaise

¼ cup slivered almonds
¼ cup chopped cucumber
¼ teaspoon ginger

Combine all ingredients mix well. Use as a sandwich filling using your favorite bread.

ITALIAN HERO SANDWICH

12 sweet Italian sausages
¼ cup water
2 medium onions

5 green or red peppers
2 tablespoons olive oil
4 hard rolls, about 5 inches long

1. In a large skillet place sausage add ¼ cup water. Simmer covered, 5 minutes. Remove cover and continue cooking about 15 minutes longer or until sausages are browned, turning occasionally.

2. Meanwhile, slice onions into thin rings then cut seeded peppers into 1½ inch strips. In hot oil in another large skillet sauté onions until just limp, then add peppers and continue cooking over medium heat, stirring occasionally until peppers are tender. Add cooked sausage.

3. Split hard rolls in half lengthwise. Top bottom part of each roll with some of pepper and onion mixture, next 3 of the sausages, then top part of roll. For easier eating, cut each roll crosswise in halves. Makes 4 sandwiches.

FRANKFURTER ~ EGG SALAD BUNS

4 split frankfurter buns
4 frankfurters, finely chopped
3 hard cooked eggs, coarsely chopped
3 tablespoons chili sauce
⅛ teaspoon pepper

1 teaspoon prepared mustard
½ teaspoon minced onion
salt to taste
1 tablespoon snipped parsley (optional)

Split and toast four frankfurter buns in broiler until golden.

Meanwhile, in medium bowl combine finely chopped frankfurters, coarsely chopped hard cooked eggs, chili sauce, pepper, prepared mustard, minced onion and salt to taste.

Spoon mixture onto split buns. Garnish with snipped parsley, if desired.

X ~ October ~ Fireside Snacks

FRIENDSHIP
The first general rule for friendship is to be a friend, to be open,
natural, interested;
the second rule is to take time for friendship. Friendship,
after all, is what life is finally about. Everything material
and professional exists in the end for persons.

~ Nels F.S. Ferre

OCTOBER ~ FIRESIDE SNACKS

October is here; the weather is changing; soon we will have to again be inside looking for ways to entertain our friends and family by the warm fire inside. This is the month that is the beginning of a season that brings a mixture of the last warm weather, cold weather, and then finally the leaves turning colors of golden orange, red and yellow. It is a time to spend outside raking leaves and watching the beauty of nature around us before the cold and wet weather again becomes a reality.

What I have for many years called "Indian Summer" is one of my favorite times of year when the weather is changing from one season to the next. In Washington State we are fortunate to have a definite change in the weather when everything changes, and it seems as though trees, plants, and some animals drift off for the winter and then again return in the spring to start all over again.

Fall is the time for casual entertaining and getting together with friends to enjoy the football season and root for your favorite team. Lots of times an impromptu gathering of friends means having lots of snack type foods, nothing that takes a lot of time and preparation. Be creative and fix an assortment of snacks that you know will be enjoyed by all. Following are suggestions that are very easy to prepare and will make a hit with your guests whether it is a prearranged gathering, or just friends dropping in for an evening of fun. You can have these snacks on hand for your own family and bring them out for unexpected company. If there is no football, bring out the board games or a deck of cards and have fun spending an evening at home with friends or family.

LITTLE PIZZAS

½ English muffin toasted	1 teaspoon parmesan cheese
1 teaspoon tomato sauce	1 tablespoon shredded mozzarella cheese
pinch Italian seasoning	½ teaspoon olive oil
1 slice pepperoni	

Spread muffin with tomato sauce. Sprinkle with seasoning. Cover with Mozzarella, 1 slice pepperoni, and sprinkle with parmesan and ½ teaspoon oil. Microwave for 20 seconds or until cheese melts.

TANGY EGG SPREAD

4 minced hard cooked eggs	1 teaspoon Worcestershire sauce
3 strips crisp bacon (crumbled)	¼ cup mayonnaise
1 teaspoon prepared horseradish	¼ teaspoon salt
1 teaspoon minced onion	

Mix together all ingredients. Spread on crackers.

OLIVE NUT SPREAD

¼ cup salted almonds
¼ cup stuffed olives

3 tablespoons mayonnaise
1 teaspoon French dressing

Put all the ingredients into a blender and blend at Hi speed until coarsely chopped. Serve on crackers.

CRAB MOLD

1 envelope unflavored gelatin
3 teaspoons water
1 can cream of celery soup
1 (3 ounce) package softened cream cheese

8 ounces fresh or canned crab
(or shrimp meat)
3 chopped green onions
1 cup mayonnaise
salt to taste

Mix gelatin with 3 teaspoons water, heat undiluted soup and sprinkle with gelatin. Remove from heat and mix in remaining ingredients. Pour into mold and refrigerate several hours or overnight. Garnish as desired and serve with crackers.

CLAM DIP

2 teaspoons prepared horseradish
1 teaspoon lemon juice

1 (3 ounce) package cream cheese
1 can minced or chopped clams

Mix horseradish and lemon juice with cream cheese. Add teaspoon of clam juice from the can then blend into cheese mixture. Add drained clams and additional clam juice if necessary to reach desired consistency. Serve with chips.

FUDGE

2 tablespoons butter
⅔ cup undiluted evaporated milk
1⅔ cups sugar
½ teaspoon salt

2 cups miniature marshmallows
1 (6 ounce) package chocolate chips
1 teaspoon vanilla
½ cup chopped nuts

Combine butter, evaporated milk, sugar and salt in saucepan over medium heat. Stirring constantly, bring to a full boil. Cook 4 to 5 minutes, stirring constantly, remove from heat. Stir in marshmallows, chocolate pieces, vanilla, and nuts. Stir vigorously for 1 minute until marshmallow melts and blends in. Pour into 8 inch square buttered pan. Cool then cut into squares.

LEMON BARS

¾ cup butter
1½ cups flour

½ cup powdered sugar

Mix like piecrust until it crumbles. Pat into an 8x8 inch pan. Bake 20 minutes at 350°.

3 eggs
1 cup sugar
3 tablespoons flour
3 tablespoons butter, softened

1 lemon
2 teaspoons zest of lemon
powdered sugar, if desired

While baking crust mix 3 slightly beaten eggs, 1 cup granulated sugar, 3 tablespoons flour, juice and zest of lemon. Pour over the crust and bake 20 minutes longer at 350°. Remove from oven and sprinkle with powdered sugar if desired. Cut into squares while warm. Cool before removing from pan.

ZUCCHINI DROP COOKIES

1 cup grated zucchini
1 teaspoon soda
1 cup sugar
½ cup shortening
1 egg beaten

1 cup chopped nuts
1 cup raisins
1 teaspoon cinnamon
½ teaspoon cloves
½ teaspoon salt

Beat thoroughly the zucchini, soda, sugar and shortening until creamy. Add egg and beat well. Add sifted dry ingredients with nuts and raisins. Drop by spoonful on greased baking sheet. Bake at 375° 12 to 15 minutes.

MINCEMEAT COOKIES

1½ cups flour
1½ teaspoons baking soda

½ cup chopped nuts
½ cup mincemeat

Sift together flour and baking soda, add chopped nuts and mincemeat.

Put into a blender:

¼ cup water
2 eggs
⅓ cup shortening
¾ cup brown sugar firmly packed

1½ teaspoon cinnamon
¼ teaspoon nutmeg
½ teaspoon salt

Pour blended mixture into flour and stir until mixed. Drop by teaspoon on greased cookie sheet. Bake at 375° for 10 minutes. Remove from cookie sheet and place on a wire rack.

TACOS

12 cooked taco shells
1 pound ground beef
¼ cup chopped onion
½ teaspoon chili powder
8 ounces tomato sauce

1 cup chopped tomato
1 cup shredded lettuce
⅓ cup cheddar cheese, shredded
bottled taco sauce

Heat taco shells as directed.

Brown ground beef and onion in frying pan. Add chili powder to taste. Drain off extra fat. Stir in tomato sauce and bring to a boil.

Reduce heat. Cook 10-15 minutes, stirring occasionally, until mixture is dry and crumbly.

Fill each heated taco shell with about 2 tablespoons of meat mixture.

Mix tomato, lettuce and cheese. Spoon 2 tablespoons over beef in each taco shell. Add taco sauce to your taste.

XI ~ NOVEMBER ~ HOLIDAY TRADITIONS

If at first you don't succeed try again. The word
impossible is not in my dictionary

~ Napolean Bonaparte

NOVEMBER ~ HOLIDAY TRADITIONS

Now that November is here, we start to think of our faith, family, and friends and begin to plan for sharing time and being with those we love and enjoy being with. First it is Thanksgiving dinner where we gather with family and friends to give thanks for where we are in life, family, friends, neighbors and all that we have been blessed with in life. Then it is time to plan for the festive holiday season following Thanksgiving. This is a very special time, and we need to plan ahead for whatever our activities will be so that we are not rushed, and can enjoy all the festivities that happen this time of year.

Most of the recipes in the book thus far can be used for the holidays, plus many have favorite recipes that are handed down in families from generation to generation. The recipes should be included when entertaining as a reminder of the past and how much the families enjoyed the meals based on recipes passed down. Following are just a few recipes that have been passed down in my family and families of friends, and some that my children have fond memories of being served at holiday dinners in our home.

SWEET POTATOES OR YAMS

Sweet potatoes, tart apples, fresh cranberries, brown sugar, apple, orange or cranberry juice.

The amount of each ingredient depends on how many are being served, and your own taste preferences.

Peel and cut the sweet potatoes and apples into eighths and place in a square baking dish. Then place the cranberries on top and sprinkle with brown sugar. Pour about ¼ cup juice over all, and bake in a 350° oven until the sweet potatoes are done.

MINCE PIE

Mince pie was always a favorite, my mom made her own mincemeat, but now you can just buy it in a jar and use your own piecrust. I like to add a sliced Granny Smith apple before baking the pie. The apple is a good combination with mincemeat for a slightly tart taste. Prepare crust for a two crust pie. Put the first crust in the pie pan, then put the filling. Top with the other crust. Bake according to instructions on mincemeat jar.

SWEET POTATO CASSEROLE

4 medium sweet potatoes   **1 tablespoon butter**
¼ cup orange juice   **2 tablespoons chopped walnuts**
¼ teaspoon nutmeg

Cook whole sweet potatoes in boiling water 25 to 30 minutes or until tender. Meanwhile, lightly spray a 1 quart casserole dish with cooking spray.

Remove potatoes from heat and add cold water until they are cool. Drain, peel and mash the potatoes. Add remaining ingredients and mix thoroughly. Place in casserole dish and bake uncovered at 375° for 25 minutes. Serve hot.

CRANBERRY ~ SAUCED GRAPEFRUIT

1 cup sugar   **2 cups cranberries**
1 cup water   **3 grapefruits, pared and sectioned**

In saucepan combine sugar and water stir to dissolve sugar. Heat to boiling and boil 5 minutes. Add cranberries and cook until skins pop, about 5 minutes more. Remove from heat and chill. Pour cranberry mixture over grapefruit sections in sherbet glasses.

CRANBERRY CHUTNEY

1 pound cranberries   **Grated rind of 1 lemon**
Juice of lemon   **1 cup packed brown sugar**
½ cup golden raisins   **1 medium onion chopped**
1 cup water   **Dash of cayenne pepper**
1 teaspoon salt   **½ cup orange marmalade**
1 tablespoon finely chopped
  crystallized ginger

Combine all ingredients, except cayenne and marmalade. Bring to boil and simmer uncovered, stirring occasionally, for 10 minutes or until cranberries are tender and liquid begins to thicken. Add remaining ingredients and chill. Serve with turkey or chicken.

CRANBERRY NUTBREAD

½ cup butter
½ cup packed light brown sugar
¼ cup orange marmalade
¾ cup small curd creamed
   cottage cheese
2 eggs
grated rind of 1 lemon
grated rind of 1 orange
¼ cup orange juice
glaze

2⅔ cups flour
3 teaspoons baking powder
1 teaspoon baking soda
1 teaspoon salt
¼ teaspoon pumpkin pie spice
1 cup golden raisins
1 cup cranberries, halved
1 cup coarsely chopped pecans or other nuts

First beat butter and brown sugar until fluffy. Add orange marmalade, cottage cheese, eggs, lemon and orange rinds, and mix well. Mix flour, baking powder, baking soda, salt and pumpkin pie spice in a separate bowl and stir into creamed mixture. Fold in raisins, cranberries and nuts. Spread in well greased 9x5x3 inch loaf pan and bake at 325° 1 hour and 15 minutes. Brush with glaze as bread comes from oven. Let stand on cake rack 10 minutes, and then remove from pan to rack to cool. Can be frozen.

GLAZE

Mix until smooth 1 cup confectioner's sugar, 1 tablespoon melted butter and 2 tablespoons orange juice (or enough to make a rather thin glaze.)

CRANBERRY PIE

1½ cups finely crushed gingersnaps
   (whirl in blender)
2 tablespoons sugar
¼ cup butter, softened
1 can whole cranberry sauce
1 cup raisins
1 tablespoon cornstarch

¼ teaspoon nutmeg
⅛ teaspoon salt
1 cup heavy cream
2 tablespoons orange juice
1 tablespoon lemon juice
1 tablespoon grated orange rind

Mix gingersnaps and sugar. Add butter and blend with fingers. Line greased 9 inch pie pan with the crumbs pressing well against sides of pan. Bake in moderate oven 350° about 10 minutes: cool. Mix next 5 ingredients in saucepan and cook stirring 2 minutes or until clear and slightly thickened, cool. Whip cream and fold into cranberry mixture with remaining ingredients. Pour into pie shell and chill several hours.

MOLASSES COOKIE CUT-OUTS

½ cup sugar
½ cup light molasses
½ cup shortening
1 egg yolk
2 cups flour
½ teaspoon soda
1 teaspoon baking powder

1 teaspoon cloves
½ teaspoon nutmeg
½ teaspoon salt
½ teaspoon baking soda
1 teaspoon ginger
1½ teaspoons cinnamon

Mix sugar, molasses, and shortening until creamy. Add egg yolk; beat well. Blend in dry ingredients. Sift dry ingredients first. Then roll out dough and cut with favorite cookie cutters. Place on ungreased cookie sheet. Bake 350° 8 to 10 minutes.

XII ~ December ~ Encourage Your Children To Be Creative

Our hearts grow tender with childhood memories and love of
kindred, and we are better throughout the year for having,
in spirit, become a child again at Christmas-time.

~ Laura Ingalls Wilder

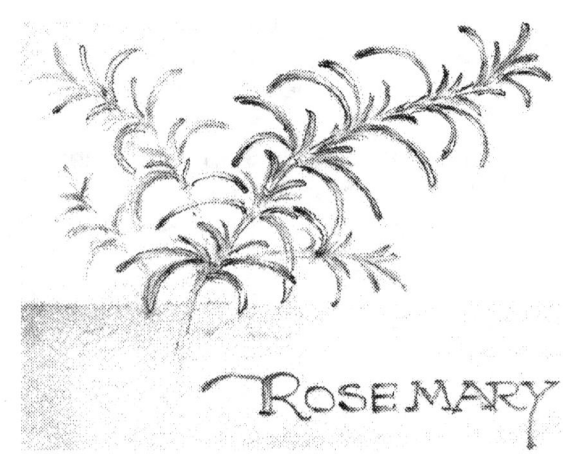

Rosemary

Now is the time to think about what we can give as a token of our appreciation to family and friends. Our children especially need guidance in this direction; they need to learn that whatever the gift is it does not have to be expensive. It can be a gift that they have designed or made using their creativity. There are so many ways to be creative, experimenting in the kitchen can be one of them. It is important to encourage our children to use what capabilities they have to be creative and share their talents with others.

Following are some recipes for crafts and some recipes for making something special for the children to enjoy eating. Take time to enjoy activities with your children, it is important not to get caught in the mode of being too busy to enjoy time spent with family.

CRAFTS

CRAFT DOUGH
CRAFT RECIPE FOR CRAFT USE ONLY

4 cups flour
1 cup salt
1 cup cool water

1. Mix the four and salt together
2. Slowly add the water and mix. Press into a ball.
3. Knead the dough with clean hands for 5 minutes.

Now shape the dough into a basket.

1. Using shortening grease the outside of a metal or glass bowl that can be put in to the oven. Be sure the bowl is well greased. Place the bowl on the counter upside down.

2. Roll some of the dough with a rolling pin until it is ½ inch thick and about 1 foot long.

3. Cut the dough into strips about ¾ of an inch wide. Put a layer of strips across the bowl ½ inch apart.

4. Now interweave a layer of strips in the opposite direction.

5. Twist one long rope of the dough to make a lip around the bottom edge of the basket to hold the ends. This will be the top when finished.

6. Brush the entire basket with about ¼ cup milk. This makes a golden brown color after it is baked.

7. Still upside down put the bowl in an oven preheated to 350°. Bake until well browned, ½ to 1 hour. (To save energy do this at the same time food for a meal is baking.)

8. Remove the basket from the oven. Let it cool before you try to remove it from the bowl. Your basket can hold bread or dried flowers.

SALT DOUGH
CRAFT RECIPE FOR CRAFT USE ONLY

food coloring   **3 cups flour**
1 cup water   **1 cup salt**

Add food coloring to water. In a large mixing bowl stir together the flour and salt. Add water mixture and stir until flour is moistened.

Turn dough out onto lightly floured surface and knead until smooth. Place dough in a plastic bag that can be sealed. Store in refrigerator until ready to use. While working with dough, keep unused portion covered with a damp cloth or sealed in bag. After you have made your dough creatures set in hot sun or bake in 325° oven until hard. Check after 20 minutes then check every five minutes or so until done. Use your imagination to create whatever you want.

CORNSTARCH CLAY
CRAFT RECIPE FOR CRAFT USE ONLY

1 cup cornstarch   **1½ cups water**
1 one pound box baking soda

In large pan, mix cornstarch and baking soda. Gradually add water. Cook and stir the mixture occasionally over low heat until it gets bubbly and thickens. Remove from heat and turn out onto a piece of foil. Let set until cool enough to handle.

This clay will keep in the refrigerator for several days. If you want to keep it longer put it in the freezer. This is a good clay to use for Christmas ornaments to put on the tree.

SALT PAINT
CRAFT RECIPE FOR CRAFT USE ONLY

½ cup salt   **Food coloring or tempera paint**
1 tablespoon water   **2 tablespoons liquid starch**

Stir together salt, water and coloring, then add liquid starch. This paint must be stirred often during use. It will give you a sparkly look. Paint a rock, or try it on some of your dried clay creations.

GINGERBREAD HOUSES

This time of year it is fun to make gingerbread houses for decorations in the house for the month of December. This is a project that can be the theme for a great holiday party. First I will include the recipe for the house pieces, and the mortar glue that holds them together.

RECIPE FOR THE HOUSE PIECES

⅓ cup soft shortening   1 teaspoon salt
1 cup brown sugar (packed)   1 teaspoon allspice
1½ cups dark molasses   1 teaspoon ginger
⅔ cup cold water   1 teaspoon cloves
6-7 cups flour   1 teaspoon cinnamon
2 teaspoons baking soda

Mix shortening, brown sugar and molasses thoroughly. Stir in water. Blend all dry ingredients and combine with moist ingredients. Chill dough.

Cut shapes for the house pieces out of paper and label each piece. Use a sheet of 1 inch graph paper to make design. You will probably need an adult or older brother or sister to do this. Preheat oven to 325°. Roll dough on floured board and cut each piece out of the dough. Carefully transfer each piece to a lightly greased baking sheet. Bake for 5 minutes. (They should have spread out a little on the baking sheet and still be soft.) Remove baking sheet from the oven and using the paper pieces as a guide, quickly but carefully trim each piece and remove the excess bits of dough that you cut away. Return the baking sheet to the oven and let the pieces bake until they are nice and dry ~ very well done but not burned. Let the pieces cool on a flat surface.

You can bake the gingerbread pieces ahead of time and store them in a dry place. Just be sure they are kept flat. Do not freeze them; this will cause the mortar not to set.

INSTRUCTONS FOR PUTTING A GINGERBREAD HOUSE TOGETHER

1. Using the pattern below cut house pieces out of parchment paper to the size that your house will be.

2. When the gingerbread is ready carefully lay out the patterns cutting one piece at a time.

3. Working with the front and sides of the house first, generously apply the icing glue along adjoining sides. (It is best to use a pastry bag fitted with a medium tip, but you can also use a spatula.) Hold the walls upright while the icing hardens. Repeat with remaining sides.

4. Once the sides are firmly together, liberally apply icing glue to bottom edges. Attach house framework to the cardboard base. Let icing harden.

5. Next, apply the roof. For best results apply the icing glue to top; edges of side, front and back walls. Apply icing glue along peak of roof. Gently press roof pieces in place. Allow icing to harden well before decorating.

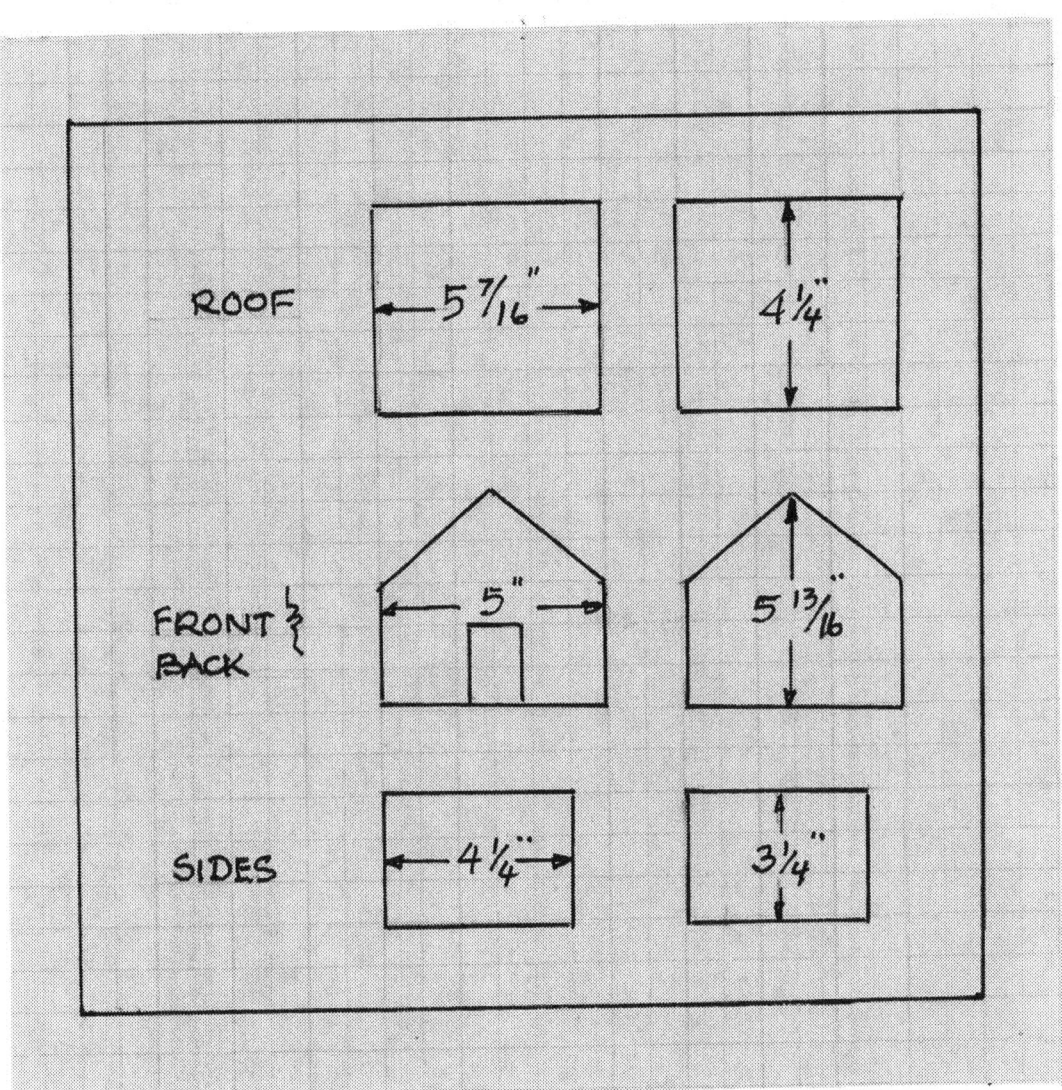

3 eggs whites
1 pound powdered sugar
½ teaspoon cream of tartar

Combine ingredients and beat for 10 to 12 minutes.
(Make sure you beat it for the correct length of time.)
The icing sets in 5-10 minutes so cover tightly when not in use. It will store well in an airtight container.

Build your house on cardboard that has been covered with foil. Assemble the walls and roof and allow time for the icing to set and become very hard before you decorate it with candies and icing.

When ready to decorate be sure to have plenty of M&M's, lifesavers, small marshmallows, pretzels, licorice pieces and whips, and any other small candies that would be good for decorating.

If making houses with a group of children you may use graham crackers as a base for the house. Carefully break the graham crackers to shape the house you are making.

If you are having a holiday party to make gingerbread houses while the houses are drying it would be a good time to serve refreshments. Then plan to have a contest and prizes for the houses.

This activity can be the start of a great family tradition. Each year as the family, or group of friends, grows and matures the houses will take on new and interesting designs.

What ever you do, enjoy and have fun. The houses make great centerpieces for a festive holiday table.

CREATIVE EATING

DINOSAUR EGGS

4 hard cooked eggs   **1 package Kool-Aid**
3 cups cool water

Gently crack the eggs until they are covered with fine cracks. Do not remove shell.
Stir together water and Kool-Aid. Add cracked eggs. Cover with clear plastic wrap and set
in the refrigerator for one day.

Remove from Kool-Aid. Throw away the Kool-Aid mixture. Carefully peel the shell from the
eggs and see the design that comes through, then you can eat these dino eggs. Experiment
with different flavors of Kool-Aid.

MUD PIE CAKE

1 gallon zip lock bag   **1 teaspoon baking soda**
1½ cups flour   **1 tablespoon vinegar**
1 cup sugar   **1 teaspoon vanilla**
¼ cup unsweetened cocoa   **⅓ cup cooking oil**
½ teaspoon salt   **1 cup water**

Put the flour sugar, cocoa, salt and soda into the bag. Seal tight and shake to mix well. Open
the bag and pour into an ungreased 8x8 inch pan. Make a well in the middle with a fork Mix
the vinegar and vanilla in measuring cup, and pour into the well. Pour the oil and water into
the well. Using a fork, stir all ingredients until they are mixed. With the help of an adult, put
the cake into the oven to bake at 350° for 35 to 40 minutes. Use hot pads to remove from
the oven. Cool the pan on the wire cooling rack. If desired can be frosted when cool. It is
also good served with a spoonful of whipping cream or ice cream when cool, or try covering
with strawberries.

SEA CREATURE SALAD

Pear	**raisins**
peach	**carrot**

LOBSTER:

Have an adult help you cut the pear in half. To make the lobster put half a pear on a small plate. Cut the peach into slices. Put one slice on the bottom to make the lobster tail. For the lobster' claws, place two more peach slices near the large end of the pear halves. Use raisins for the eyes.

Have an adult help you cut the carrot into thin sticks. Decorate the lobster with small sticks of carrots for the antenna and mouth. Decorate the shell with slices of carrots or raisins, if desired.

FISH

Put a pear half on a plate. Use peach slices to make the fins and tail of the fish. Add carrot strips and a raisin for the eye. A piece of carrot can be cut to form the mouth.

OCTOPUS

Use a peach half for the body of the octopus. Make a face with raisins. Have an adult help you cut long curls, or slices of carrots to use for the eight tentacles.

Use your imagination to decorate Sea Creatures in different ways. Fresh or canned fruits can be used.

MICROWAVE BREAD PUDDING

3 slices bread	**½ cup raisins**
3 eggs	**½ cup brown sugar**
1 teaspoon vanilla	**¼ teaspoon salt**
1 – 12 ounce can evaporated milk	**1 teaspoon cinnamon**

Butter bread. Beat eggs with vanilla and milk, then add raisins. Layer bread in 1½ quart casserole. Sprinkle sugar, salt, and cinnamon over the bread. Pour milk over the bread. Cover and bake 8 minutes on high. Let stand for 10 minutes.

HELPFUL HINTS

This section is an added bonus for those who like innovative ways to solve a few everyday problems. These hints will help avoid some simple problems we have in everyday life.

Button all buttons on clothing and turn inside out before putting into the washer. Fewer buttons will fall off and the garments will fade less if turned inside out.

To clean an automatic washing machine, fill washer with hot water and add one gallon distilled vinegar. Let the washing machine run the full cycle (no clothes in it.) Do this about every six months, cuts down washing powder and mineral deposit residue.

According to washing machine repairmen, most washer breakdowns come from overloading. Know your washer capacity and do not overload.

Run a cup of white vinegar through the entire cycle in an empty dishwasher to remove all soap film.

When repairing a scratch in furniture always rub with the grain of the wood.

To help lessen scratches in furniture, remove the meat from a fresh walnut or pecan. Break it in half and rub the scratch with the broken side of the nut.

For all minor scratches in wood, cover each scratch with a generous amount of white petroleum jelly. Allow the jelly to remain on the furniture for 24 hours then rub into wood. Remove excess and polish as usual.

For larger scratches, fill by rubbing with a wax stick (available in all colors at your hardware or paint store) or a crayon that matches the finish of the wood.

To remove paper that is stuck to a wood surface do not scrape with a knife. Pour any salad oil, a few drops at a time, on the paper. Let set for a while and rub with a soft cloth. Repeat the procedure until the paper is completely gone.

Old decals can be removed easily by painting them with several coats of white vinegar. Give the vinegar time to soak in, and then gently scrape off.

For sparkling clean chrome without streaks, use a cloth dampened in ammonia.

Cement glue can be removed by rubbing with cold cream, peanut butter, or salad oil.

To remove the sticky residue after taking off price tags on pans, plastic or leather goods, rub a little peanut butter into the spot. The peanut butter will also work if you need to remove residue from an adhesive bandage.

To remove the "ouch" when removing adhesive tape from your skin, saturate a piece of cotton with baby oil and rub over the tape. The tape will come right off without burning the skin.

Spray garbage bags with ammonia to prevent dogs from tearing the bags before they are picked up.

A cheap brand of lawn fertilizer will melt snow and ice just as quickly as salt. It will benefit your lawn instead of killing it.

Pop your contact paper into the freezer an hour before using it and it will handle much easier.

When the tip of your shoelace comes off, dip the end of the lace in clear fingernail polish and let dry. You will have a hard-tipped shoestring again for easier lacing.

Organize a toy lending library, or swap toys with other mothers in the neighborhood.

To rid a cutting board of onion, garlic or fish smell, cut a lime or lemon in half and rub the surface with the cut side of the fruit.

COOKING DEFINITIONS

AL DENTE ~ Spaghetti that is cooked but still firm.

BOIL ~ To heat liquids until bubbles form that cannot be stirred down. In the case of water, the temperature will reach 212° at sea level.

BREADING ~ A coating of fine breadcrumbs or crackers used on meat, fish and vegetables.

BROIL ~ To cook meat 4 to 6 inches from a heat source, usually a broiler in the oven.

BROWN ~ To cook food in a small amount of fat over medium to high heat until the food becomes brown sealing in the juices.

CHOP ~ To cut foods into ¼ to ½ inch pieces.

COAT ~ To dip or roll foods in flour, sugar, or a sauce until covered.

COMBINE ~ To place several ingredients in a single bowl or container and thoroughly mix.

CORE ~ To remove the seed area of an apple or pear using a coring tool or a small knife.

CREAM ~ To beat butter, margarine or shortening with sugar, using a spoon or mixer until light and fluffy.

CRISP-TENDER ~ Defines vegetables that are cooked until they are crunchy, yet tender enough to be pierced with a fork.

CUBE ~ To cut foods into ½ inch to 1 inch pieces that are square in shape.

CUT IN ~ To break down butter, margarine or solid shortening into a flour mixture using a pastry blender or two knives.

DASH ~ Less than ⅛ teaspoon to measure salt, spices, herbs. Not an accurate measurement.

DICE ~ To cut foods into small cubes ⅛ inch to ¼ inch in size.

DOT ~ To break up small pieces of butter and distribute over the top of a dish or casserole.

DRIZZLE ~ To slowly spoon or pour a thin stream of an icing, melted butter or other liquid over food.

FILLET ~ A boneless piece of fish, chicken, or meat.

FOLD ~ Combine light or delicate ingredients such as whipped cream or egg whites with other ingredients without beating. A rubber spatula is used to cut down through the ingredients, move across the bottom of the bowl and bring up part of the mixture. Just to combine the ingredients, not mix them.

GARNISH ~ To decorate or embellish with parsley, or whatever you wish to decorate with.

GLAZE ~ To coat with a thin glossy mixture.

GRATE ~ To rub foods, such as hard cheese, carrots, potatoes, etc., over a grater to produce fine particles.

GREASE ~ To coat the inside of a baking dish or pan with fat to keep the contents from sticking.,

HULL ~ To remove the green stem and leaves of strawberries.

JULIENNE ~ To cut foods into long thin matchstick shapes about 2 inches long and ¼ inch thick.

KNEAD ~ To work foods, usually dough, by using a pressing and folding action to make it smooth and elastic. Push with the palms of your hands and pull or fold back with your fingers.

LINE ~ To cover a baking sheet with a piece of waxed or parchment paper or foil to prevent sticking.

MARINATE ~ Place meat or raw vegetables in a liquid mixture of oil, vinegar, wine, lime, or lemon juice, fresh herbs or garlic. This will tenderize and flavor foods.

Mince ~ Cut foods into very fine pieces no larger than ⅛ inch. Used often for fresh herbs or garlic.

MIX ~ To stir or beat two or more ingredients together with a spoon or a fork until well combined.

MOISTEN ~ Add enough liquid to dry ingredients while stirring gently to make a wet but not runny mixture. Often used in the preparation of muffins.

PARBOIL ~ Boil foods, usually vegetables, until partially cooked.

PAR/PEEL ~ Remove skin from fruits and vegetables using a small knife or vegetable peeler.

PARTIALLY SET ~ The consistency of gelatin when fruits, vegetables, and nuts can be added without floating.

PINCH ~ A small amount (less than ⅛ teaspoon) of a seasoning or spice that can easily be held between the thumb and index finger. This is not an accurate measurement.

POACH ~ To cook meat, fish, eggs, or fruits in simmering liquid.

PUREE ~ Mash solid foods into a smooth mixture using a food processor, food mill, blender or sieve.

REDUCE ~ Thicken sauces and gravy by boiling down and evaporating a portion of the liquid in an uncovered pan.

SAUTE` ~ Cook or lightly brown foods in butter, margarine or oil until tender.

SEPARATE ~ Divide eggs into whites and yellows.

SIFT ~ Put dry ingredient into a sifter to remove lumps, this adds air and combines dry ingredients.

SIMMER ~ Cook liquids alone or a combination of ingredients with liquid just under the boiling point. (180° to 200°)

SOFTEN ~ Bring butter, margarine, cream cheese or ice cream to a soft consistency by leaving at room temperature for a short period of time.

STEAM ~ Cook foods, covered, on a rack or in a steamer basket over a small amount of boiling water. Most often used for vegetables.

STIR ~ Blend a combination of ingredients by hand using a spoon in a circular motion.

STOCK ~ Long simmered broth made from meat, poultry, fish and/or vegetables with herbs and spices.

STRAIN ~ Separate solids from liquid by pouring through a colander or sieve.

THREAD ~ Place pieces of meat and vegetable onto skewers when making kabobs. This is also used for fruits.

TOSS ~ Quickly and gently mix ingredients with a spoon and fork. Often used in salads or pasta dishes.

WARM ~ Hold foods at low temperature without further cooking, usually 200°.

WHIP ~ Beat rapidly by hand or with an electric mixer to add air and increase volume.

WHISK ~ A multi-looped wire mixing utensil with a handle used to whip sauces, eggs, cream salad dressings, etc., to a smooth airy consistency.

ZEST (PEEL) ~ The outer portion of a citrus fruit. Remove zest or peel, use a small sharp knife, a grater, a vegetable peeler or a special gadget called a zester.

KITCHEN RULES

When creating in the kitchen it is important to have an adult or mature friend, brother or sister helping. There are some things in the kitchen that do need to be supervised. Cooking on a hot range, using the oven, using a blender or mixer and when using a sharp knife are times when there should be an adult or mature person present. Remember, using common sense in the kitchen is very important.

When using the oven be sure to know if your oven is hotter, or cooler, than the temperature required. Some ovens are not exact when it comes to temperature; you can check it with a meat thermometer. This will allow you to make any necessary adjustments, if needed. When baking time is given as a range, like 10 – 15 minutes, always check the earliest time first.

ALWAYS REMEMBER

Always clean up the kitchen, leaving it shining for the next person who will be using it. When preparing food it is always wise to have the sink filled with warm soapy water. When finished using a utensil place it in the sink. This really makes cleaning up a lot easier.

Always turn the burners on the stove off when not in use and when finished turn the oven off.

SPECIAL FOOD NEEDS

Many people have special food requirements for whatever the reason. When you have guests over for dinner or just to relax, it is always good if you can accommodate specail dietary needs in the food selections. The internet or a library provide great resources if you are not sure what to prepare.

One of the most important things about special food needs is that the person concerned stays on their diet so that no complications arise because of not following their diet. Whenever you entertain someone with special needs, make sure there is enough variety of foods to meet the needs of your guest. Many times a guest will offer to bring something special that they can eat. If this is the case, graciously accept the offer. When entertaining don't make an issue of the needs of others, just incorporate those needs in what you plan to serve.

With any special food need it is important to read labels and be sure you know what is in any product that you serve. For information on recipes the health food stores are great resources, and the internet is full of recipes and information about anything that you might want to know. Don't be afraid to just jump in and do research on what the needs are, there is really a lot of information. All you have to do is look.

Remember when you invite someone over for a meal make sure to ask if there is any food that they have to stay away from. Planning any meal is important, but when you have guests you want to include a variety of foods so that everyone invited will find something to eat and have a relaxing and fun experience in your home.

INDEX

Italian Cheese Dressing (January) 4
Marinated Carrots (January) 5
Molded Cucumber Salad (January) 6
Overnight Lettuce Salad (January) 7
Picnic Potato Salad (January) 6
Pineapple Cheese Mold (March) 23
Sea Food Salad (January) 6
Spinach Apple Salad (March) 24
Spinach Salad (January) 5
Yankee Doodle Salad (January) 7
Zesty French Dressing (January) 4

Creamy Zucchini (June) 41
Garden Casserole (June) 40
Meatless Side Dish (March) 20
Mushroom Casserole (June) 41
Parmesan Zucchini Frittas (June) 40
Spaghetti Squash (March) 22
Sweet and Sour Zucchini (March) 22
Sweet Potatoes or Yams (November) 72
Sweet Potato Casserole (November) 73

SAUCES AND TOPPINGS (July)

Banana Nut Sauce for Ice Cream (July) 49
Basic Sauce for Ice Cream (July) 49
Bleu Cheese Basting Sauce (July) 51
Cranberry Glaze for BBQ Chicken (July) 52
Fresh Pineapple Sauce for Ice
    Cream (July) 49
Fresh Strawberry Sauce for
    Ice Cream (July) 49
Lemon Barbecue Sauce (July) 51
Lemon Parsley Sauce (July) 51
Plum Sauce for Ice Cream (July) 49
Raspberry Sauce (July) 21
Sauce for Hotdogs (July) 52
Seafood Sauce (March) 21
Tomato Mustard Sauce (July) 51

SOUPS AND STEWS

Lentil Barley Stew (March) 19
Vegetable Soup (March) 20

SPECIAL FOOD NEEDS 90

VEGETABLES (July)

Cheddar Cheese and Zucchini (July) 50

RECIPES AND NOTES

_____

_____

_____

_____

_____

_____

_____

_____

_____

_____

_____

_____

_____

_____

_____

_____

_____

_____

_____

_____

_____

_____

_____

_____

RECIPES AND NOTES

RECIPES AND NOTES

RECIPES AND NOTES

RECIPES AND NOTES

_____

_____

_____

_____

_____

_____

_____

_____

_____

_____

_____

_____

_____

_____

_____

_____

_____

_____

_____

_____

_____